UPLIFT

OBSERVATIONS OF AN INTROSPECTIVE NATURE

BC COWLING

Edited by Kate Seger
Interior Design by Eli Neff Akridge
Cover Design by Eli Neff Akridge

www.bccowling.com

CONTENTS

PREFACE

Most of us desire a better life, but how do we go about creating one? Haphazardly for the most part in my experience.

My passions override my common sense too often, turning stepping stones into hurdles. Most of us learn from experience, and I am no exception. Repeating an experience because I did not learn it the first—or tenth—time is not uncommon in my life.

My father wanted me to look like the student council kids he saw at the Merry Go Round Restaurant in Evansville, Indiana. Did he look like their parents? Did he act like their parents? Not even close.

My dad was a creative, flawed, near-genius who resisted maturing with a passion. He simply did what he wanted to do throughout his life.

In his late twenties, he worked for his father and uncle in our family's furniture store. When modern furniture and interior decorating took hold in the late 1940s, Dad redesigned the third floor of the store into a then-futuristic group of model showrooms with 1950s rich muted colors.

By the mid-1960s, when I was in high school, Dad continued to dress in these same rich interior decorating tones. He would wear a pale green crew neck mohair sweater with mustard slacks, matching socks, and dark green loafers set off with a subtly striped Fox Brothers sport coat. Everyday attire for Dad.

I came home in the afternoons during high school about the time Dad was getting up and went with him to his favorite nearby cafeteria for his breakfast and my afternoon meal. Dad worked at night writing big band jazz, or designing Formula Five racing cars, or being a collector's stamp dealer. His work evolved over the years.

Dad was not alone in having his "Do As I Say, Not As I Do" moments. Did I learn from Dad's request to be like the other kids? No, because the way he lived showed me a much different picture. My experience of the example he set was more meaningful to me than his words.

Why then am I writing this collection of unsolicited advice?" Writing makes me feel more alive, so I do it whenever I can, uplifting my life.

I also have learned that upon occasion, someone's words will highlight a step about to be taken by another person and prove helpful, possibly uplifting.

For myself, one element of learning is deciding what is useful and what is not. As you read through my thoughts and experiences, please disregard whatever you feel is irrelevant to your life. If anything written here is useful to you, then I am doubly rewarded.

I wrote many of these chapters twenty-five years ago. As I reviewed and edited (thanks Kate!) this manuscript, I considered updating references from that past time but decided against it for the most part. I have updated how long ago events occurred. The essence of each chapter is more important than the details of the stories. Hopefully, you will agree.

1

ADVICE I EMBRACED

MY CHOICE

Half a lifetime ago, my then-girlfriend changed my life. Jane and I sat in the kitchen in her San Francisco apartment, planning a winter trip to Mexico. I needed to be warm. I had just returned from visiting friends in the Midwest. Jane was about to quit her job to travel with me, hoping to find her art once again. As I sat looking across the white kitchen table at her, I felt she was the person I needed to be happy. Describing to her how I had felt trapped and fearful on my recent trip back to Illinois, I wallowed in the bad feelings. She listened patiently, then said, "It feels to me that you like being unhappy. Happiness is a choice. If you do not choose to be happy, you never will be."

Jane was right—and her timing was terrific, for I was open to the truth in her words. I found that I could make the choice to be happy. Choosing happiness has not proven to be easy, but Jane gave me the awareness that I have the power to do so. For this experience alone—and we shared many other wonderful moments —I will always be grateful to her. We lived in Mexico for five months, returned to San Francisco, struggled through the summer, and finally decided we could not resolve our fundamental differences. I moved to Hawaii two months later, still seeking warmth.

Why was I able to take the step Jane offered me that day in her kitchen? And why is choosing happiness a constant challenge? Training and habit are my answers. I had grown enough spiritually in the previous few years, opening my awareness to be able to see the truth Jane offered. I had trained myself to take that step. Training is a continual part of life if we are to learn and grow. We have many teachers, but through our choices we guide our own training. Whether we take long bumpy roads or direct paths is our continual choice.

What about habit? Is it your habit to grumble and focus on pain and misery? Many people like to commiserate. Negativity is easy, comforting, and self-perpetuating. Being downcast requires less effort than being upbeat. Both positive and negative choices gain momentum in their separate directions for myself as I repeat them. And like so many ironies in my life, the choice which begins easy soon turns hard. How many times have you avoided a difficult but constructive choice and found yourself later in a more stressful situation because you did not deal with your business-at-hand earlier?

The positive choice that can seem difficult initially, which is so easy to avoid, usually becomes lighter with practice. Making these positive choices have led me toward light and love. The choice is each of ours to make every moment, every day. You can choose happiness!

VALUE ALL EXPERIENCE

YOURS COUNTS MOST

My father stood in front of me in the living room. He held an unopened pack of Camels in one hand and a lit Benson & Hedges in the other. The ash was about to drop off his cigarette.

"Where did these come from?" he asked, not quite yelling. The Camels had dropped out of my coat pocket. I cursed my carelessness. As a teenager, I lied to my father to avoid his anger, working hard to keep stories straight and not do anything dumb—like letting cigarettes fall out of my pocket.

"Oh...ah...I'm just keeping them for Steve, you know. His parents would freak at the sight of cigarettes. I told him I would keep them for him. I knew you wouldn't mind cigarettes being in the house."

Dad looked at me. I had been caught off guard, and my lie was transparent. "Tell Steve I do mind. I don't want you smoking, son. It is a dumb, dumb habit. Got that?"

"Right. OK," I said, relaxing. He was not going to get mad. "Dumb habit, Dad."

Handing me the Camels, his cigarette ash falling onto the carpet, he walked back into the dining room, where he was working on his Formula Five car designs. I went down the hall to my room and fell on my bed, my heart pounding. Dad's anger terrified me.

My father was good at saying, "Do as I say, not as I do!" without saying the actual words. He seemed to have given up on improving himself, but he wanted to make sure I did not make the same mistakes he made.

What did I learn from this? I lost respect for him each time his words and actions did not match. Instinctively, I still wanted to be like him, even when I disliked what he did. Rarely did I learn from his experiences, clearly not as often as he wished.

Why not? Because they were his experiences. I might see the truth in what he—or anyone—says to me, but until I experience it myself, the truth remains distant from me, a belief at best. Believing is, for me, the way I shape my approach to the issues I have yet to experience. I have learned to keep my mind and heart open as often as possible and just let it be.

I used to work so hard to avoid painful experiences, I created even more anguish for myself through the avoiding. Repeating a painful loop often before seeing the illusion I was chasing was not an uncommon occurrence in my world.

Then I would begin to peel back another veil of truth, seeing one layer deeper into myself and the world around me.

In the years since my father translated (died), I have gradually let go of the old fear associated with him. Letting go of this fear and pain helped me learn to welcome all experiences—joyful or painful, happy or sad. Sometimes the welcoming takes a lot of work. I experience growth when I take risks...constructive risks.

What am I risking? Usually, I'm just leaving something behind—something which, painful or pleasurable, has become too familiar and comfortable. Taking a step into the unknown can be scary, but I find it is always rewarding.

I learned many things from my father, including how best not to approach some situations. But nothing I learned had a real impact until I had my own experiences to digest.

I support each of us holding our own counsel in high esteem. You and only you can best define truth in your life. Do not take my word for anything. Use discrimination and look for what resonates as true to you, then try it for yourself.

Learning from experiences is one of the keys to creating happiness.

3

COMPLAINING

WHY DO WE DO THIS?

Most of us complain sometimes. Does complaining feel good? Does it attract the attention we desire? Does complaining provide a "safe" outlet for bottled up anger? Is complaining a habit?

Whatever the reason you complain, you probably are not genuinely happier because you do so. Complaining may satisfy an in-the-moment urge to vent frustrations, but what else does it accomplish?

Complaining creates negative energy, which makes more complaining easier. Without self-awareness and discipline, a small amount of complaining can lead to a nasty habit that corrodes our environment.

Complaining is like dumping garbage on your living room floor. This action might feel good at the moment when you are angry, but do you want to live with garbage in your living room?

Most people prefer to take garbage outside and put a lid on it. Then, once or twice a week, the garbage collector comes and takes the garbage away. We no longer languish in our own waste.

Since complaining is hard to see after it has been aired, it is easy to think it does not linger, stinking and offensive to the people we love. If complaining were solid matter like garbage, we would quickly see how it accumulates and its negative impact on our lives.

Complaining is an invisible, personal waste product that builds up and lingers, polluting our homes, families, friendships, work relationships, personal attractiveness—our entire lives.

A good friend of mine is married to a man with many charming qualities. This man has a kind heart, loves his children dearly, works hard, is successful, and does not fritter away time and money indulging in addictive habits. What more could she ask for?

She would like him to take responsibility for his personal waste products. This nice man complains incessantly about life in general and at his family and workers specifically. He does not accept responsibility for venting his anger and frustration. He dumps his personal garbage on those he loves most.

If you find yourself complaining, put a quarter into a jar. Next time, add two quarters to your personal fine jar. Keep increasing the amount. It won't take long to get your attention and motivate you to uplift your outlook.

Who gets the money? Whoever will handle it the best in your home.

Maybe you already have a swear jar for your teenager. Combine the two if it feels right. Or put some tape on a finger, a note on your door, or any other way to remind yourself what you want to accomplish.

Complaining tears at the fabric of our lives. The quarter in a jar approach is one method of preventing these tears. Maybe it's not the right way for you. It doesn't matter which method you choose to achieve your goal, as long as it motivates you. Anytime we focus on finding constructive ways to redirect our energy into something positive, uplifting, and constructive, we will move our life in a lighter, happier direction.

4

SMILING OFTEN

WILL OPEN YOUR HEART

The next time you are feeling low, walk down the street, through the mall, across a park—wherever you find people—and smile at everyone you see.

Some people will smile back at you; some will not. Who smiles back is not your concern, but watch people's eyes. Soon you will see someone's eyes light up with joy as they smile back at you. Your heart will open for a moment with no conditions or expectations.

Feel better? Sure you do. Smile at the cashier in the grocery store, the clerk in the gift shop, your waiter at lunch, your co-workers, your best friend, your family. Smile at everyone you meet, and inevitably you will feel better. When you are smiling, you are shaping your world. You are giving other people's words, actions, and feelings less power over you.

When I was in college studying sculpture, there was

one woman in the art department I just did not like. She was an east coast snob to me, talking to anyone who would listen about the private school she had gone to, going on unnecessarily about this great artist or that avant-garde genius whose show she had seen in SoHo. Made me want to puke. And she was my neighbor! I tried practicing neutrality and failed miserably.

One day she was walking in my direction across the campus. I would have changed direction if I had thought of doing so before it was too late. Bracing myself for one of her self-aggrandizing comments as she came closer, I was surprised that she simply smiled —a from-the-heart, open, giving smile. Then she was gone. Stunned at first, I soon let go of my many opinions of her and floated through the rest of the day, smiling.

We never became good friends, but we did smile at each other every chance we got.

Whenever you can, make smiling a habit in your life. It's warmly contagious. A smile can change a frown into a rainbow.

TAKE TIME TO TALK TO PEOPLE

TO LEARN FROM THEM

Once you are comfortable smiling at people, take a little extra time whenever you can and talk with people.

Ask the waiter at lunch what he does when he is not at work. Maybe he is a student. What does he study? Which university does he attend? By stepping outside yourself, you show another person you are interested in more than what they can do for you.

The clerk in the flower shop may share an interest in hang-gliding or knitting with you. Perhaps the clerk longs to share her excitement about getting married. You will never know unless you ask.

Stop to talk to your neighbors in the hall or on the street. They usually will not bite if you smile first. You do not have to speak long. If they invite you to have tea or a drink, go ahead if it feels right. If their invitation is not appealing to you, decline gracefully—and with a smile.

You can be a friendly neighbor without becoming buddies. You may have to learn how to set better personal boundaries. Saying "no" may make you uncomfortable, but it is a skill we all need. Discomfort usually leads to learning, then it takes us on to growing and strengthening our foundation for a better life. Facing small fears is an example of a difficult choice that becomes more comfortable with practice.

Take time to talk with people. You will be surprised at what you learn!

DRIVE NICE

YOUR CAR WILL LAST LONGER

D oes your car have a few scrapes and dents? Do other drivers glare at you, honk their horn or give you the finger? How many yellow lights do you speed through? How often are you late? Gotten any speeding tickets lately? Did you feed the meter yesterday? Have you parked in a handicapped space, no parking zone, or too close to a fire hydrant while saying to yourself, "I'll just be a minute."

When I let myself slip into any of these attitudes, I eventually realize the actions are symptoms of my anger, time management problems, and/or disrespect for others. You can probably add to the list. Most of us periodically drive with our emotions instead of our heads.

What does driving a little out of control do for us? We risk injury to our loved ones, possibly creating an instant family trauma. Hurting someone we do not know can be very hard to endure.

Driving a little out of control can cost us time and money in traffic court or at the repair shop. Do you enjoy crashing your car? I do not! And everyone's checkbooks suffer. I am much more likely to have an accident if I let my anger or haste affect my driving. Are you?

How would you feel if you parked so close to a fire hydrant your car had to be towed before the fire department could hook up their hose to fight a fire? Maybe a little girl will get badly burned because your car was in the way. Maybe your car will be damaged. The odds are against either of these events happening, but it is possible.

A high school friend of mine let his testosterone influence his driving and lost the top half of his head on his way home one night. Another friend passed someone too close on the freeway, then got caught up in a race and chase game, not realizing he had made the first offending move. The other driver's actions escalated, and miles later, he found himself trapped in a cul-de-sac with a big, menacing man coming after him. A bigger man working in his yard nearby persuaded the angry driver that my friend was not worth the bother. My friend left shaken but unhurt. Today he drives much less aggressively.

Angering other drivers by cutting in front of them or speeding by them usually does not harm us in the moment. Running the red light usually will not result in an accident. But we are taking big risks for small gains. How many minutes must we save to balance the possible harm and cost of one traffic accident?

By giving our emotions control of our driving, we lose a wonderful opportunity to take a time-out from our stress. We are passing up a chance to create a different moment for ourselves. Suppose we develop the habit of becoming gracious whenever we get into our car? We drive at safe speeds, take a moment to let another driver into traffic, park where parking is allowed, and smile at someone who glances at us.

Over time we can develop a habit of kindness. We can condition ourselves to calm down when we get into our car. Develop this habit, and then by simply getting into a car, we will help neutralize our anger of the moment, our anxiety over being late to work, or to pick up the kids. We are going to be late anyway. Why compound our problems by driving out of control?

I have learned the value of being grateful whenever someone gets in my way, slowing me down when I am rushing to somewhere. I do not know the future, but maybe, just maybe the person I want to swear at is saving me from a greater problem by a short delay. Just maybe. I don't always practice what I have learned—but I try. How about you?

7

WE ARE WHAT WE EAT

AND A WHOLE LOT MORE

I was taught in science class that our bodies generate new cells every seven years. Presuming this is true, no cell alive today in your body will be around seven years from now. On average then, about 14% of you will be regenerated in the next twelve months.

How do we manufacture your new cells? The first step is obtaining raw materials.

Our physical bodies are built and rebuilt from the raw materials we ingest. If we eat high sugar, high starch, high fat, highly processed foods, we create a weak, unhealthy body. If we eat whole grains, fresh fruits and vegetables, and healthy proteins, we will create a strong, vibrant body. Which do you prefer? No matter how healthy we feel, we are healthier and more robust if we eat less junk.

Other factors affect our health besides food.

Emotions, exercise, and environment are three. How many more can you name? Food is our building material. Our actions, thoughts, and feelings are our tools.

Many things contribute to what we experience at any given moment. Full awareness of every force affecting us would overload our minds. Just knowing, though, that our choices do have a real impact on our tomorrows is enough motivation to think again about the decisions we are about to make today.

How will getting angry affect you? Next time you are angry, ask yourself, "Is my anger really necessary? Could I find a better way to express my frustration?" Being angry is a poor way to show love. Is my anger Kind? Necessary? True?

Positive thinking advocates like to say, "You are what you think." Food and thought are potent forces in our lives. What else? Love? Does being loved affect you? Loving? The love we give out affects the love which comes back to us.

In my twenties, I began relationships by learning what my new partner needed and then giving it to them for as long as I could. When I ran out of energy, I presented them with a list of my needs—in both subtle and overt ways—and expect them to fulfill me just like I had fulfilled them. Never worked.

Why? I was giving to get. The quality of my love was need-based, far from unconditional. Thirty years later, I learned love means giving freedom and harmony is more important than being right. I experienced love as the most potent force in my universe. Being more in harmony with myself led to more harmony with those around me, creating a stronger foundation to make healthy choices about the raw materials I choose and how I assimilate them.

8

CHANGE

EMBRACING THE PROCESS

C hange or die. Life is that simple.

As a child during the 1950s, I was indoctrinated with the '50s Dream: a family, a house, two cars, and a good job. This Dream was something to work for, something to achieve. Only after attaining the Dream would I be happy.

I struggled to get "there," operating on the subliminal assumption that the Dream would then be maintenance-free once accomplished. After all, who needs change when the Dream is realized?

Gradually I unlearned this cultural illusion. Before I became aware of it, though, I defeated myself many times by looking at my challenges as hurdles to get somewhere. I did not realize change is a process. Until I learned to embrace this principle, I resisted change because I wanted to be where I thought I was going, not where I was. Today, I still relearn this lesson on occasion. The old programming faded slowly because it was an echo of a primal urge to resist pain.

Change is hard for most of us because we resist it. Our resistance is what makes change unpleasant—not the change itself. A relationship grows comfortable, perhaps stagnating in some areas. One person in the relationship goes through a transition, which disrupts the comfortable sameness for their partner. What then? People have made many different choices in this situation. Happy people usually face these changes and adapt. Or the other way around: people who embrace changes and adapt grow happier.

When we resist change, we create problems. For example, Chestnut Street used to be two-way traffic. Last year the city planning board changed Chestnut Street to one-way traffic flow. What do you do? If you do not change your driving habits on Chestnut Street, you invite the serious problem of driving the wrong way on a one-way street. Resist enough changes, and your life span may well shorten.

If we accept the need to embrace change, how can we do this more readily? Little things usually are the key. A friend shared that when she gets stuck in her writing, she tries changing things around, such as changing from a blue to a black pen, changing the time of day she writes, and/or trying a new font on her computer.

What would you like to change in your life? Maybe drink less coffee? How about using a different cup and make barley tea? Yes, you will miss the caffeine euphoria, but give it a try for a week. Maybe you will feel better.

To step into tomorrow, we need sound footing today. Embracing change helps create our solid personal foundation. Small details often hold the key.

9

GROWTH

CHANGE WITH GUIDANCE

A s important as change is, guiding change makes an even more significant difference in the quality of our lives. Without guidance, our changes can be very chaotic.

Suppose your spouse suggests you both are watching too much television. She has decided to join a book discussion group that meets two nights a week. "Would you like to come along?" she asks. When you decline, she asks you to find something to do to break the dull routine you both have gotten into at home.

You agree to find something else to do two nights a week besides staying home and watching television. You have consciously decided to change. What do you do? Go bowling? Take evening classes? Go to a bar? Get a girlfriend? Join a spousal support group? You have many choices. Which activities you choose will determine the quality of guidance you give yourself in making this change.

We are all changing, if only at the cellular level. Taking the time to consider where we are and what our next steps might bring us can have a positive impact on our lives.

I hit my personal rock bottom in San Francisco during the early 1980s. My choices over the previous ten years had caught up with me, creating a serious health problem. Though HIV was developing in people all over the city, my lifestyle spared me exposure to it. Instead, I continued to cycle through the viral syndrome I had brought with me from St. Louis.

I was changing, to be sure, but mostly in a downward spiral. Sobered by my growing inability to care for myself, I began to evaluate nearly everything in my life.

This forced introspection became the foundation for the work I did when I completely fell apart, landing in San Francisco's well-developed mental health system.

No doctor could find anything physically wrong with me, so I began therapy…lots of it. At one point while living in Baker Halfway House, I consciously began evaluating every decision I made, no matter how small. Diet, language, courtesy, activity, budgeting, attitude, physical expression, anger, listening, laughter —I kept my attention on making the best choice I could every moment.

Living in a mental health program requiring a high

level of self-focus made my task more doable. I had no job or spouse to consider. I cooked in the house only once a week.

Two years into this project of making positive choices, I experienced a spontaneous good feeling. My first. Until that moment, a good feeling was a forced outcome of finding something outside myself and trying to bring it inside. Those forced attempts to change what I was feeling did not last long and mostly generated different, not good feelings.

My old choices of booze, anger, strip clubs, women, partying—seeking something outside myself to try to feel better—were the driving force behind my downward spiral. Making better choices showed me the way to pull myself out of the deep hole I had created for myself.

10

REWINNING PERSONAL GROWTH

EVERY DAY

P ersonal growth has to be rewon every day. There is no shortcut.

During hard times in San Francisco, I was fortunate to work with an intuitive therapist. Christine offered me high-quality support and clarity, but she could not do my work for me.

A few months after I began seeing Christine, I identified my pattern of endearing myself to a woman by listening closely to her, asking questions about her experiences, and drawing out her feelings...as I mentioned earlier.

The women I became close to loved this side of me. What was not so loveable was my change after an emotional bond was established. Then I would subtly submit my "bill" of needs. My message was, "I have met your needs, now please meet mine."

When I first understood this pattern, I was confident I had solved a major hurdle. I shared my insight with Christine. She smiled.

A year later, I had a relationship with an outgoing woman. She liked my attention but was unable to give me what I wanted. I talked about this incident with Christine, who helped me see I was repeating the pattern I had "solved" the year before.

Later, when I was with my girlfriend, Jane, in San Francisco, we worked on our relationship with Christine in couples' counseling. I complained that Jane did not meet my needs. I met hers—or so I thought— why could she not meet mine? I felt mistreated. Christine led me again to my old insight, and I again faced rewinning this step.

Another personal awareness I gained was talking about people. During the summer after I met Jane, she visited me often at a hot spring north of San Francisco, where I lived and cooked. For the month of September, she lived there with me in an old cabin near the hot baths.

I had been careful to stay clear of the politics and personal gossiping that seeped through the hot springs' small population. A week after Jane joined me, I realized we were talking about people in unflattering terms. At first, I wanted to blame her. Luckily I did not, for soon, I realized I was the source of our gossip. I knew from experience that talking about another couple's problems could bring their troubles into our relationship, and I did not want to do this.

Looking deeper into my motivations, I saw I had been using other people's problems to reinforce our emotional bond.

We talked about what we were doing and decided to eliminate gossip from our conversation. The decision was easy but required constant awareness. On some days, we had to rewin our new attitude every hour.

Six months later, we faced some unpleasant results of my careless and negative comments about people we liked in Mexico. Again I had to rewin my growth in this area.

Each day some personal growth needs to be rewon. The cycles of our patterns and life circumstances vary the rhythm of when and how often different issues surface. But each day old challenges can emerge in new ways.

How do we realize we have slipped back toward a destructive habit? One key is to develop gentle self-awareness. Not so much as to push us off balance, but just enough to keep the door open to small warning signs.

Trust your instincts. Nurture your instincts. When I make a choice based on an inner nudge—intuition—I take the attitude that listening to this inner nudge is not a question good or bad, but rather a step in a life-long process of developing trust in my inner awareness. The journey is more important than reaching the destination.

The same can be said for rewinning our personal growth. The process of developing our self-awareness and listening to our instincts can help us in ways beyond the daily challenge of rewinning our personal growth.

11

CYCLES OF GROWTH AND REST

AN ART

Punish or pamper? Which do we choose most often for ourselves? Many of our choices are not so dramatic, but we all make adjustments to either speed up our efforts in a particular direction or put on the brakes.

Why do either? Why not just "be" and coast through life? Why not push ourselves every moment of every day? Some of us do better with a relaxed, casual attitude. Some of us have to push ourselves to get anything done. Some of us blend these approaches.

My college roommate Michael was a pusher. He had a large callous on one finger caused by holding his pencil very tightly since the second grade, he once told me. He was studying math and econ and routinely was at his desk with textbooks open when I went to bed. Most of the time, he was up in the morning before me, too, cooking scrambled eggs.

I spent time at his home, and I knew his parents and sister. I did not sense the forces that caused Michael to push himself away from his family. But those forces were undeniably there.

Was Michael's life balanced? On more than one occasion, he told me he did not think it was. I have not been in touch with Michael for almost twenty years. Last we spoke, he worked at a think tank in Washington DC and had been appointed to the President's Council of Economic Advisers.

Another friend lost his way completely in college and spent his last semester eating peanut butter from the jar and watching reruns all day on television.

I was somewhere in the middle of these two friends, but a long way from balanced. I worked hard and partied harder. I got my degree in sculpture and industrial arts, learning the skills I needed to build my kinetic art. My degree prepared me for a lifetime with no career training. This was my choice, and I have both paid for it and been rewarded by it many times over. My time in college strengthened a value that I learned living with my father: "What I am doing is more important than what I have." Dad would never say these words. He lived them.

Life has a natural rhythm of growth and rest. Nature reflects this principle with every passing season. Each of us feels life's rhythm a little differently. Are you in harmony with the beat of your drummer?

One way to learn about your inner rhythm is to review your recent course corrections. Do you jerk yourself back and forth by first pampering yourself after a hard day, then punishing yourself the next morning for relaxing too much? Do you often criticize yourself? Do you overeat when you get anxious? Do you make yourself work late when the project can wait until tomorrow? Do you wait until the last minute because you "work better under pressure?" Do you feel guilty when taking some downtime?

Some of us push ourselves too hard and seldom relax. Other people rarely get themselves in gear at all. Because we grow from our experiences, whatever we do is fine. Some paths are just longer than others. Pushing too hard can lengthen our personal journey as surely as doing nothing if we are not in harmony with our inner rhythm.

The better we learn to feel—and then listen to—our inner guidance, the more we can shorten our path to mastering each challenge. Relax or get moving. Knowing which approach is best for us at any given moment and then following through is an art. Learning this art will help us move toward being happy.

12

SMALL STEPS SCALE MOUNTAINS
BIG STEPS CAN BRING DOWNFALLS

For three years from 1980 to 1983, physicians prescribed antibiotics for my viral throat infections with no effect. Not willing to admit I needed to make major changes in my lifestyle before I could feel better, and, growing more desperate, I began reshaping my diet.

I read several books from health food stores. I had noticed that when I was feeling flu-like, which was happening more often, I did not feel bad while I was eating. After I finished a snack or meal, I then felt bad again, sometimes much worse. What I ate also affected how I felt, but the changes were unpredictable.

One of the first authors I read was a professor who wrote about fifty-day water fasts, soup being too watery to be nutritionally beneficial, eating as many raw foods as possible, and the benefits of enemas. Everything he wrote was radical to me.

This professor was so enthusiastic, his books so full of successful case histories, I wanted to have the great health he wrote about. But how could I fast? I felt better when I was eating. I tried some of his recipes, which were different from my normal diet, but not too different. My health improved a little. I took small steps with my diet but felt unsatisfied with my efforts to feel better.

When I moved to San Francisco from St. Louis in April 1983, I drained my savings. I felt the pressure to find work, but reestablishing my handyman business in a new city required patience. Repairing homes gave me the freedom I craved. In May, I found some work. Before the first job was done, I had a second, then a third job. By sticking to my new diet, I felt strong enough to work.

In June, I had to return to St. Louis for my bankruptcy hearing in an effort to protect my building while trying to sell it. The ongoing viral infections had wrecked my cash flow. My cousin John, an attorney, was kind enough to represent me at no charge, but I was required to appear at the hearing.

My emotions swung wildly, and I was unable to maintain my diet while traveling. A week later, I returned to San Francisco to find the work I thought was waiting for me had been done by someone else.

Weaker and more desperate, I plunged back into my search for health and work. I read books with other approaches to eating, many of them conflicting with each other. I passed out my Handyman Service flyers and called on property management companies. The work momentum I had created was difficult to reestablish, but I did find some small jobs.

I also jumped into a raw foods diet, frantic to regain my good health. Within ten days, my energy soared. Throughout July, life held new promise. I was almost current with my rent, and my roommate was not pressuring me.

During this time and against my inner nudges, I let myself be pulled into a spiritual group. On the first of August, I realized the spiritual group was not for me, and I abruptly pulled out of it.

My reoccurring flu-like symptoms returned. I panicked. My financial life could have withstood a dip in health, but my emotions could not. Overreacting, I went to a restaurant in the Fillmore District and ate a hamburger, fries and drank two beers.

Burgers and beers do not usually make people sick. After weeks of raw foods and a then-undiagnosed liver condition from past alcohol excesses, the meal was catastrophic for me. I became very sick.

Weeks later, struggling to work at all and falling behind in my rent, I let myself get severely chilled in San Francisco's ever-changing weather. I became sicker yet.

Five years passed before I earned another dollar. Years later, I have yet to fully recover my health. What happened? I tried to take too many big steps. I tried to change too much at once in my life. Extremes have always held an attraction for me. Excitement is addicting. Gradually I began to understand myself better. I realized that small, often unexciting steps are a better path.

A commodities trader once told me he was successful because of his training as a pilot. The preflight checklist could never be rushed. He transferred this discipline to his trading and to avoid getting emotionally involved looking for a financial home run. He was content and profitable hitting singles. Small steps.

13

VISUALIZE

WE ALL DO IT

W hen you describe a house, a car, a person —anything—you visualize what or whom you are describing. Visualizing is a powerful tool that can be even more useful with some self-training. By visualizing, we can bring a new job or relationship into our lives, a change in our health, material possessions—the possibilities are endless.

If you are curious or adventurous, spend a few minutes each day or evening and sit quietly. Whenever possible, choose the same time and place each day. Close your eyes and imagine one way in which your life could be better. Contemplate on what you are imagining. Do this daily for a month, then change your image to a different way you hope to improve your life.

Visualizing is as simple as focusing on what you want and as complicated as creating a host of unseen disruptions in your life. As with most tools, there are hazards.

A former roommate of mine belonged to a religious sect that practiced a particular chant. She was excited about her chanting because she said it brought into her life the things she asked for while chanting. We occasionally talked about her experiences, and she was open about using this religious practice to get material goods. This woman was visualizing.

What my chanting friend was not aware of was the effect of her actions. If I want more money and I rob a bank, I will have more money and more problems. We can easily see the effects of robbing a bank. The action of robbing the bank is a physical world event and is the cause of unpleasant effects.

Most of life is unseen. Can you see love, anger, or creativity? You can see the results, but not the feelings. Cause and Effect, also called "Karma," is part of our lives. We reap what we sow. What goes around comes around. You get back what you give out. These phrases are a part of our language. Even if bank robbers are not caught, they have set in motion a cause that will come back to them in some form.

How did my chanting roommate create unseen problems for herself? She put her will ahead of Spirit's (God by any name) will. Had she first declared, "If it is for the good of the whole and in the best interest of my spiritual unfolding, then I would like..." she would have saved herself troubles that she probably will never relate to her chanting and the things it brings into her life. She likely would receive fewer things, but what she brought into her life would be free of a hidden price.

Visualization works more than most of us imagine. By learning to use this tool and manage it with responsibility and persistence, visualization can help each of us on our path toward a fuller life.

14

PROBLEMS ARE OPPORTUNITIES

TREAT THEM LIKE VISITING RELATIVES

W e all have problems. What would life be without them? "Oh, great!" you say. "I would welcome life without problems!" Are you sure? Would you be the person you are today without the hurdles you have faced in your life?

As much as I would like a problem-free life, I have gradually recognized that my life's purpose is to mature, grow, and be of service. Without problems, I would grow little. Hanging onto a problem unnecessarily, though, is neither fun nor productive. How do we avoid prolonging problems, and how best can we utilize the difficulties in our lives?

I like to treat problems like visiting friends or relatives. The more I resent a problem, the more uncomfortable it becomes. So I work to accept problems as they surface, to acknowledge that the unpleasantness of the moment has arrived to help me grow.

If not-so-close friends show up unannounced the weekend you were planning a family campout, you probably will debate between being flexible or bluntly honest. You could decide to delay your camping trip a day and give your full attention to your friends with the understanding that they are on their own for the rest of the weekend. Maybe you provide them with a key to your home Saturday afternoon as you leave. Perhaps you tell them of a lovely bed and breakfast a short drive away. Either way, you solved your problem with a minimum of stress by giving the issue the space it requires without surrendering your world to it.

If a problem pops up with a business associate, give it some space. Leave the situation at work so it will not affect the evening with your family. The next day, take a look at the problem from a new perspective. You may see the issue in a better light. You may discover a solution that did not occur to you the day before.

When we give our problems respect, attention, the space they require, and refrain from hanging on to them, they have a better chance to resolve. When we have learned what a problem has to teach us, it will leave our lives, uplifting us in a small way, and making room for our next opportunity.

15

GRATITUDE

THE BEST ATTITUDE

W hat is gratitude? Most of us know gratitude as what we experience when we have just avoided something terrible.

During spring break from graduate school, I drove from St. Louis to Colorado on I-70 to see my girlfriend, Dee. A fourteen-hour drive in reasonable conditions, my goal was twelve hours. A winter storm warning did not alter my plans.

As I crossed the state line into Colorado, I noticed more snow on the side of the road, but the interstate roadway looked clear. On the downhill side of gently rolling terrain, I approached a line of cars going slower than highway speeds. I passed cars on my right then braked in plenty of time to slow as I approached the first car in the left lane directly ahead of me. I did not slow down. Pumping the brakes frantically did nothing.

Instead, a dump truck changed lanes right in front of me. My heart in my mouth I yelled like crazy, still pumping the brakes without effect. Moments before I was about to smash my old Pontiac station wagon into the truck, the driver lifted his bed just enough for the tailgate to crack open, allowing a thin layer of sand to spill on the road in front of me. My tires grabbed, and I slowed to a safe speed. My heart rate gradually returned to normal.

This county truck was sanding the roadway! I was the fool who almost caused a major collision on a cold, snowy day. This was my introduction to black ice and a reacquaintance with a level of gratitude I had not felt for a long time.

I was grateful to be alive and had not injured others. My heart opened deeply with a love for life that carried me the rest of the way to Colorado.

Dee and I had a tender middle-of-the-night reunion that survived her distress at me showing up a full day earlier than planned. My enthusiasm to see Dee had blinded me to her situation and feelings. When I left Colorado four months earlier Dee had taken over the lease of my upstairs apartment. There had been no landlord walk through or a formal turning over of the unit. I still had house keys. As close as Dee and I had been we had not commitment to a monogamous relationship. We had not discussed it. I could have walked in on Dee in bed with a new boyfriend. Yikes!

Gratitude opens my heart, but clearly does not improve my decision making.

When we are filled with gratitude, there is no room in our consciousness for negative qualities that close our hearts. Can you be angry, can you complain, can you be afraid while you are grateful? Yes, we mix emotions, but the more gratitude we feel, the less room we have for darker feelings. I have experienced being filled with gratitude for as long as a weekend. The feeling was incredible. I wish I could live fully immersed in gratitude.

Why do we often wait until a near-tragedy to feel grateful? Most of us have not trained ourselves to shape our feelings. Our feelings are by-products of our actions, words, and thoughts. To live in a state of gratitude requires consistent attention. When I get upset with someone, I usually blind myself to a bigger perspective. I lose the awareness that I am here to grow, mature, and serve. Everything I encounter can teach me something if I am open to learning, but it is easy for me to get stuck in a moment's negative qualities.

The earth is a place of both positive and negative energy. We can choose to focus on our troubles, or we can look for what we have in our lives that uplifts us.

How can we nurture our gratitude? We could list the people, the qualities in ourselves, and the things in our life for which we are grateful. By reviewing and updating our list periodically, we remind ourselves to think about someone or something on our "Grateful List."

Visualize yourself being grateful. Train yourself to consciously chose to be grateful. The more we are grateful, the more our hearts will open and the better our life will be.

16

NURTURE YOURSELF

A MOST UNSELFISH THING TO DO

If we do not nurture ourselves, who will? Parents nurture their children with the quality varying widely. No matter how well or how poorly we are nurtured as children, though, at some point in our lives, we become responsible for our own nurturing.

Most of us struggle with self-nurturing. We either resist the concept or are unsure how best to give ourselves what we need. My father did not teach me responsibility. When I wrecked the family car, he yelled at me, then got our car fixed. When my best friend, Tim, had an accident, his father made sure no one was hurt, then sat down with Tim and helped him plan how he would fix the car. Tim learned how much work his mistake caused him. I learned for the thousandth time how horrible my father's anger felt. My Dad was not a bad man. He just had not learned to nurture himself. He was a sea of unmet needs, and he looked at those around him to meet his needs. When I goofed, he got angry, but as soon as his anger dissipated, he immediately wanted a return to our closeness, leaving him unable to discipline me in a structured way. I learned about the downside of neglecting self-nurturing by watching my father.

The quality of what we can give to others is determined by the quality of what we give ourselves. By nurturing ourselves, we fill our cup and can then easily share with another. If our cup is leaky or unfilled, we have little to share.

If your son's passion is cross-country skiing and you have nurtured yourself by regularly exercising and eating healthy foods, you probably will have a great time skiing with him. If you work to understand and manage your emotions you will be able to offer quality support to family and friends.

Some of us do not care for ourselves well because we prefer to take care of someone else. We avoid working on our problems by saying we do not have the time, energy, or money. We then serve as poor role models for the people we so wish to help grow. Some of us shy away from doing something for ourselves because it will "hurt" someone. Usually, the "someone" is hurt because they are too self-involved to see beyond their own world.

I watched my father work hard at his passions. Whether writing music, building model trains, manufacturing racing karts, or buying and selling collectible stamps, his work focus was tremendous. I had to develop my discipline before approaching my father's commitment level, but I knew what I was working toward because my father was a great role model for me in this area. He nurtured his work life.

Look for ways that you need nurturing, then make an effort to provide for yourself. The people around you will soon recognize how you have changed for the better. Their eyes may show their feelings first.

17

LAUGHTER

HUMOR YOURSELF

Many years ago, my mentor in the mortgage business would pour positive energy into the company nearly every day. He uplifted all of us who worked with him. Riding on the crest of this strong current of love was his cheerful smile and ready laugh.

Sometimes we laughed at him. Bob was full of ideas and not shy about trying them, even if he looked a fool. No closer to perfection than the rest of us, Bob treated himself with humor often enough to win our affection.

When my wife and I deadlock on a contentious issue, eventually, one of us will smile and say something funny, usually at our own expense. Neither of us can remain angry when the other person makes fun of themselves.

Laughter lightens any situation. Laughter opens our hearts as quickly as gratefulness and is often easier to find within ourselves. Can you remain depressed when you watch a funny movie?

Norman Cousins wrote about laughing himself out of cancer. Bob also healed himself from cancer with traditional and alternative medicine plus a triple dose of positive thinking and laughter.

Laughter can be damaging, though, if it conceals anger. During my twenties, I laughed at other peoples' weaknesses. Making fun in a not-so-nice way was one of the few ways my family found acceptable to express anger. Almost all other expressions of upset brought a huge helping of criticism down on my head.

When I moved out of my father's home, I unleashed my pent-up anger in ways I had learned were socially acceptable at home. After ten years of being habitually catty, I realized several friendships had a hollow ring to them. They were hollowed out by my negative comments..

With some work and a lot of help, I changed, though even now, years later, I still must guard against my old habit.

When we laughed at Bob, or myself, or anyone else in our office, we laughed with that person, at their humorous side, which mirrored our humanity. Joyous laughter is a positive energy that builds on itself. Negative energy, including spiteful laughter, destroys the fabric of our lives. Since laughter lightens your life, laugh as often as you can in an uplifting way.

18

CHILDLIKE

MORE FUN THAN CHILDISH

D o you know any adults who are reluctant to have fun?

Perhaps you hesitate to be as spontaneous as you once were. Why? As children, most of us played with abandon, creating imaginary worlds to entertain ourselves and our friends. Carnivals, movies, new adventures were all fun and exciting. Do you have fun as easily today as you did as a child? Most of us would have to say "no." Why? What happened?

We grew older, got jobs, and had children of our own. We either became responsible adults or felt the added pressure of meeting our obligations when not being responsible. We felt our parents' expectations, then developed our ideas of what we should be. We heard that big boys and girls do not cry, so we stuffed our feelings away. Systematically most of us were trained to repress our happy, care-free, childlike natures.

What did this training accomplish? Two things that I have observed: 1) we developed the outward appearance of being adults, and 2) we had a lot less fun. Many of us completely forgot how to have fun and lost our childlike lightness. We leaned on the numbing effects of television or the distortions of alcohol and drugs to be entertained.

Why is fun important? Fun opens the heart. People with open hearts live better and are kinder to each other. The more someone's heart is open, the more love can come into this world and be shared with the people they care about.

Being childlike is possible even as an adult. Yes, some balance is needed. As adults, we are responsible for caring for ourselves and our families. Responsibility does not suppress our natural, childlike qualities, but our resistance to responsibility does.

When we are unhappy with our life, temporarily escaping our discomfort is often just a step away. We usually do not realize that by taking this step, we are running away from the world we have created. Our escape is childish, not childlike.

In our effort to be responsible adults, we may repress instead of run away from our discomfort. In doing so, we quash our happy, childlike nature. Acting childish is often confused with being childlike. Childish actions are motivated by desire and fear. Childlike behavior is a natural spontaneity that uplifts anyone who allows their heart to open.

When I first met a previous girlfriend, she did not know how to have fun. Her life had become too serious. Little by little, she learned to loosen up. Now she can go to a game arcade and play air hockey or have video races, laughing whether she wins or not.

She limited herself because her adult experiences had compromised her childlike spontaneity. Childlike behavior is contagious and takes many forms. A common element, I believe, is having an open, pure heart, if only for the moment.

Among the adults in my little guy world, only my grandfather would get down on the floor with me to play. We built cool forts together from my Uncle Bob's elaborate set of shaped wooden blocks. My grandfather was a pure heart. He died when I was seven. Light and love were diminished in his home, where my sister and I lived.

Literally half of our small town of 8,000 people came to his funeral. My father sobbed for an hour that he had never told his dad he loved him. My grandmother went to bed for a week with a migraine, adrift without her Robert. Both of them had been nourished with granddad's love, but neither learned to open themselves to their own childlike joy.

Granddad was special. He had a love for others that he shared without reservation. We all have our spark of God within us if we let it shine forth. Being childlike does not require playing on the floor or going to an arcade. We simply need to open to the wonder and playfulness in each of us, whatever forms that takes in the moment.

19

DO A GOOD DEED EVERYDAY

ANONYMOUSLY OR FOR A STRANGER

What do we have to lose by doing a good deed? Is our time so precious we cannot find three minutes a day to help another person? Are all the people we meet in such good shape they need no assistance, no matter how small? Are we so happy with our life today we no longer need another person's smile to warm our hearts?

Doing kind things for the people we love is one of the ways we express love. Sometimes the people in our lives know what we do for them. Sometimes they do not. Sometimes we tell them, sometimes we do not. I am sure my father did many things for me I did not know about. He was also good at pointing out how a particular effort of his was for my benefit. Usually, these words of his felt more like control and less like a gift.

Doing a good deed every day anonymously or for a stranger is an exercise. Like working out physically, this exercise requires effort and discipline. Only a small amount of time and energy is required, and the enrichment we can bring to our life is amazing.

Cut some flowers from your garden and leave a bouquet attached to your neighbor's doorknob. Ask your co-worker if you can bring them anything when you go out to run an errand. Bring the office secretary her favorite muffin or drink when you return from lunch. Maybe you will get lucky, and she will be on break, and you can leave an anonymous note. To find opportunities like these, you only have to look for them.

Spreading kindness will brighten our world, but doing so just to get something back will not. Giving to get is an easy attitude to slip into if we are overly focused on ourselves.

I have caught myself doing for others while thinking about what a nice person I am and what they might do for me. To work my way out of this self-involvement, I visualize uplifting energy pouring through my heart. When I do the homework to open my heart and move my little, needy self out of the way, I feel a special kind of love come through and watch it bring happiness where it shines.

This special love does not have the desires or needs of romantic love. This love uplifts in a pure way that asks nothing in return. To me, it feels like the divine love of Spirit.

Take a few minutes each day to make an effort to do a good deed and watch your life brighten.

20

INTEGRITY

I COULD NOT BUY IT

Finagling has always come easy to me. Well into my adult life, it was open season to maneuver through whatever was happening any way I could. Living with my father, I learned as long as I did not upset him or get arrested, I had a wide latitude of choices to solve problems.

Lying to my father to avoid his anger was one solution. This childhood survival pattern worked for me until I learned I did not have to answer the exact question he asked. He was sharp, so my deflections had to be subtle, but half the truth often worked better than all of it.

As a teenager, I took an hour-long trip with Dad's friend, whom I did not know well. I found myself lying to this man about things that did not matter to either of us in our brief time together. That day I realized I had lost control of my lying. Wondering who else I had lied to automatically, I promised myself I would change my behavior...except when Dad was likely to get mad.

That afternoon ride down Indiana Highway 41 with a near-stranger was the beginning of establishing my personal integrity. I had a sense of what integrity was but would have struggled to define it at age sixteen.

We learn much of our behavior from watching our parents. As we slowly gain more control over our lives, we become more accountable for our choices. A lie I told my father to avoid his anger when I was young did not impact my life the way lying to a friend or client would as an adult.

Early in the summer of 1992, I decided it was time to buy a new car. My business world was beginning to stabilize, my credit was improving, and I was tired of driving my no-frills economy car. I became excited over an Acura Integra and decided to buy a two-year-old model. Since I owed as much on my older car as I could sell it for and had little cash in the bank, I could only hope to qualify for a lease, which did not require a down payment.

I found just the car I wanted. The 1990 white, 4-speed hatchback Integra LS had only 12,000 miles on it and was priced right. Only one company in Honolulu provided leasing for used cars. I reviewed my income taxes and current paystub and decided I probably would not qualify.

Feeling full of myself from recently closing several loans for mortgage clients (without finagling), I decided to discreetly modify my income documentation to show more income than I had made. Who would know? I convinced myself I had "earned" the newer car.

Like most of us, having decided to buy a particular car, I saw the same model everywhere. Curiously I always came up behind these Acuras, or they overtook me on the highway. Rarely did I see the front of the cars, just the backend.

The leasing company gave me verbal approval to buy the car but delayed issuing final, written approval for ever-changing reasons. After three weeks of waiting, I was officially turned down.

Laying in bed the night my financing fell through, I kept seeing "INTEGRA" written boldly across the back of a car as it moved away from me. Finally, the message became clear. By lying about my income, I had compromised my integrity. I had stumbled in my twenty-five-year-long effort to develop good integrity. Laughing at myself, I thought about how long it might take to work off the effects of my actions and sensed I would be keeping my economy car for quite a while.

Today I define integrity as saying what you mean, doing what you say, and always—always—update the other party if you cannot do what you said you would do, before the event if at all possible.

How do you define integrity? How important is it to you?

21

YOU, ME, AND CONFRONTATION

THE MIRROR PRINCIPLE

W hen you are upset with a friend, lover, or someone at work, what do you do? Many of us talk to ourselves instead of talking to the other person. If we do talk to the other person, we often do not talk about what is really bothering us. When we finally talk about what is upsetting us, we often make the situation worse by the way we talk about it.

Some years ago, I became upset with my then-girlfriend because she was late one evening. We were both late occasionally. I wanted to complain because I was upset she had made plans to visit her sister in California two weeks earlier but had just now told me. I did not want to put my feelings on the table because then I would have to look at why I was upset. My true motivations lay mixed between wanting to be more a part of her life and being unhappy about being left behind. I did not want to talk or think about either of those feelings.

How did I express my anger to my girlfriend? I said to her, "You're late!" After she defended herself, I said, "You are inconsiderate. You are rude. You are unkind." We had a lively evening before one of us laughed at our craziness, and I then apologized.

Today I am better about being responsible for my feelings and try hard not to ask those close to me to adjust to my weaknesses.

We all have core issues that bother us. Life is never going to be smooth. Sometimes we lose it. Knowing that I could not handle my feelings this particular evening with my girlfriend, what could have made it easier?

I had learned about "you" statements from more than one counselor. When I said to my girlfriend, "You are inconsiderate," I was attacking her. I declared battle, and the issue became secondary. She felt attacked and defended herself without apology.

If I had said, "When you are this late, I feel taken for granted," she probably would have told me how sorry she was and explained what had happened to make her late. Why? I would be making myself vulnerable by opening my heart and expressing my feelings.

Whenever I find myself beginning statements with "You," whether to someone else or to myself about someone else, I know this is a red flag. I may choose to ignore the warning, but I will eventually have to take responsibility for what I am doing...and the sooner, the better.

At times I had become annoyed when this girlfriend was short-tempered with strangers in public. Her behavior and my reaction puzzled me. Then I heard about the Mirror Principle, which says, "We are upset by other people doing what we need to work on ourselves." When people reflect to us the parts of ourselves we do not like, it is upsetting.

I am sometimes rude to people, which I do not like to admit. When a girlfriend—or anyone—exhibits the same behavior I want to suppress in myself, they push a button of mine. I react. The key to this puzzle for me is awareness. The more I can keep my awareness focused, the more I can learn from my reactions.

Replacing volatile "You" statements with expressions of our feelings and looking inside ourselves when another person annoys us are two ways to better handle some of life's speed bumps.

Becoming more proficient at saying what is bothering us in a way that leads to discussion, harmony, and smiles makes working through the next problem much easier. Handling our irritations better instead of spewing them around our world reduces conflict. The better we handle conflict, the less we avoid it, and the more clearly and more in the moment we can live.

22

LIFE IS NOT FAIR

WHO SAID IT WAS?

Did anyone tell you life was fair? Regardless of what we have been told, most of us believe that life should be fair, and to whatever degree it is not fair is an injustice.

Is there a bigger picture to life? Most of us would agree that there is a higher power of some kind and that we probably are not aware of everything which affects us.

Have you lived before? Does life start and stop with this lifetime? How many seemingly unexplainable events occur every day? Some people say, "We only live once, and if you do not believe this, you will go to hell." Other people say, "We live many lives both here in the physical plane and in the higher worlds. If there is a hell, it is life on Earth compared to the higher spiritual worlds."

What is right? Does it matter? What is important to

me is what will help me live this life better. Those arguing about right and wrong are like school children fighting about who gets on the bus first while the bus drives away.

What can help you live your life better? Only you can decide that. If you are at all like me, what worked last week or last year may not work as well today.

More and more in my life, I trust my intuition, which I call my inner guidance. I began by trusting this guidance about spiritual matters, then expanded the trust to every day life. I have learned to trust when something echoes true in my heart. I do not ask anyone else to take it as their truth. I also deflect people who tell me what I should believe.

I believe in a higher power—God by any name—and that I have lived many lives in other bodies before this one here on earth. I also believe I lived lives without my physical body in the higher spiritual worlds and that most, if not all, other Souls have done the same.

Why do I believe this? First, this belief echoes true in my heart. Second, I have had glimpses into some of my past lives. Third, the principles of Karma and Reincarnation explain to me why many things that happen in our lives appear unfair.

I do not ask anyone to believe I know about some of my past lives. But for a moment, assume with me that each of us has lived many lives. Assume that each of us is fully responsible for everything we think, do, feel, and say—all our choices. This is not the responsibility brought on by fear or as punishment. There is no one to punish us in a spiritual sense. The responsibility comes from creating our world through the results of our choices in all our past lives. We live what we create. If we are to be punished, our punishment comes from having to live the life we created. Everything we set in motion will be neutralized sometime, by some future choice of ours. This is the principle of Karma.

What we carry with us today, our unneutralized results, is our Karma.

Countless things happen in my life that cannot be explained when I look at this lifetime as my first and only visit to Earth. But when I look at this lifetime as just another day in the third grade, life makes more sense to me. There have been many days of school before this one, and many more will come afterward. Life for me is to learn and to become a better person. I have also repeatedly proven that I am pretty good at mucking-up things.

If Karma and Reincarnation are true, what do you think the next life will be like, as an example, for the German Nazis of World War II infamy? A child crippled from birth may be crippled because, in a former life, that Soul crippled other people. Whether the crippled child was a Nazi in its past life is not our concern. However, if we allow for this "unseen justice," then life becomes suddenly fair and much more intriguing. The justice is each creating our own lives. It would be clear to us if we could see all our past choices that are affecting our current lifetime.

Our business is not to judge others. Even if we knew

for a fact the crippled child had been a Nazi, the child is still as deserving of our compassion as any Soul.

I believe we create our own worlds. I have no one else to blame. I take responsibility for my own experiences. With this attitude, whatever happens to me can only be fair. I found this approach improved my life, no matter what else I believe.

If I create my own world, then I can change it. If I can change my world, then I can create more freedom for myself. Embracing responsibility creates freedom. Embracing total responsibility creates total freedom.

Just because I want to change my life, can I do it immediately? If I am in New York City and want to be in San Francisco, can I beam myself there, Scotty? No, I must prepare for the trip and earn the right to act on my choice. If I do not have the money to fly, the car to drive, or the time and the health to hitchhike, I will not see San Francisco.

Deciding I want to go is the first step. Creating the reality of going may take a while. Changing my life works like traveling from New York to San Francisco; the variables are just more wide-ranging.

Take a broader view of life, allow for the unknown, be compassionate and non-judgmental toward others, and see where this attitude takes you.

23

LIVING IN THE MOMENT

MAKE THE MOST OF IT

Where do you live? Do you live in the past, in the future, or in the here and now? Most of us would answer, "I live here, in this moment. Where else could I live?" We live, truly live, wherever we direct our attention.

In the funeral home the evening before my father's funeral, my Aunt and Uncle stood by my side before his open casket. We were the only ones in the room. My Uncle had just flown in from the East Coast. He had not seen his brother for several years. When he and his sister, my Aunt, turned to go, they were not aware of me standing there. They were not in that moment. They were remembering their brother, my father, as he had been when alive—remembering all of him, both loving and unpleasant.

When my Aunt and Uncle left the room, I laid down

on the floor and just wailed like a baby. I was nearly thirty, but I felt like I was five. "Why did you do it, Dad? Why did you do it, Dad?" I knew why he had taken his life, but the awareness was not comforting that evening.

I pulled myself back together and walked to the door of the room. My Aunt and Uncle were just coming back for me. "Sorry, Sport," my Uncle said, "Didn't mean to forget you." My Aunt put her arm around me. None of us were living in the moment that evening. I am not sure anyone would be.

When I have ended a heartbreaking relationship, I could not be fully in the moment for quite a while. Strong emotion pulls us out of ourselves. Movies and music make millions of dollars because of this principle.

After my father died, I lived in his home for nine months sorting through his many belongings and remodeling the house to sell. During those months, I worked through much of my pain and anger with my father, but not all of it. For several years memories of him intruded into my thoughts. For me, this was a good thing because I was processing old pain. This step was necessary for me to heal. Had I continued holding on to him, though, I would have handicapped my life.

In big and small ways, we can become caught up holding onto memories and pain—or longing for the future so much we are not fully in the present. In my childhood's unhappier times, I wanted to be older and be in control of my life. I lived only partially in the moment.

Watching my friends and family, I see many of us holding onto our longing to escape from something. Doing this robs us of our life, to a small or large degree. Beginning a new relationship is very hard if you are still holding on to your former partner. Studying for an exam is impossible if you are daydreaming about playing baseball the next afternoon.

Staying in the moment is not valued by all. Our culture sells emotion. Getting somebody to feel and then act in a certain way is the goal of most advertisements. Emotions are created either by evoking the past to sell nostalgia or by showing us how our lives would be better if we bought a new gadget.

Learning to be in the moment can free us from being programmed by our emotions. We can still feel. Knowing that we have feelings, but are not them, frees us to manage a part of ourselves that so often manages us.

I have found that developing a healthy neutrality toward much of life lays a foundation for learning to guide feelings. Neutrality is not indifference but rather accepting life beyond what we can change in any given moment.

When a crisis is looming, do you tie yourself up in knots worrying about what will happen, or are you free to experience your life as you choose? When I get stuck about something, I have learned to ask myself, "100 years from now, will this matter?" Invariably the answer is, "No." This little phrase is a great tool for me to balance fear in the moment, though I must be careful not to use it to rationalize escape.

Once you are more aware of your choices, the next step is to learn the discipline needed to consciously shape your life. Living more fully in the moment whenever possible is one way to accomplish this goal.

24

GOALS PROVIDE DIRECTION

FOCUS ON THE PROCESS

As a young man, I struggled with trying to become something other than myself. I graduated from high school a semester early because I was bored with school and wanted desperately to be away from home. My high school counselor was reluctant to let me graduate early, so I fabricated a story about my father and I moving to England.

I was accepted at the small college my father and mother had attended, but permission to enroll early, in the middle of the year, did not arrive until a week before I needed to be there.

My father was against me going to college in mid-term. When he had gone to the same school, being a part of the class of '43 had been very important to him. I did not care whether I was in the class of '72 or '71.5; I just wanted to go.

The day before I was to leave, my father came into my room and again asked me not to go but told me the decision was mine. Sitting next to me in my small room, our knees touching, he began to cry softly. Seeing tears roll down his cheek, I knew I could not leave him. He had just gone through a difficult divorce with my step-mother and was working hard to get his Formula Five racing car business off the ground.

So I put off the goal of mine to get away to college as sons as possible in order to be with my father. I did reach the goal nine months later, but by then, it was old news.

At the end of high school and during my first year of college, I wanted to be a psychologist. My freshman psychology class was boring, so I skipped it regularly and stayed at our apartment to write. After a few weeks living in a fraternity house, I had moved in with a senior class English major.

Becoming a writer captured my imagination. I read Kurt Vonnegut and J. D. Salinger while writing awful short stories. At the beginning of the spring semester, I learned I had flunked all my finals the semester before and was asked to leave school. More plans became ashes.

Two years later, I tried college again as a declared writing major. One class showed me that I had nothing of interest to say. During the same time, I was taking an acting class. Becoming a professional actor became my new goal. For two years, I was utterly immersed in theater. Able to emote in avant-garde plays, I felt I had talent. By the end of the two years, however, I knew I could not act. I could not become another person, even for the short time a production requires.

Bailing out of school, I read D. H. Lawrence and worked at a picture framing shop. By working with my hands, I discovered a new side of myself. A year later, I was building sculpture and studying art. I did get an undergraduate art degree, but my plans to teach were derailed when I was pushed out of graduate school by the sculpture professor who was insulted when I would not submit to his drunken power games. Another plan became roadkill.

Frustration built up in me each time I "failed." From art school, I went into the business of building sculpture, though I spent more time working on first one studio, then a second when I was forced to move. My father's death interrupted my pursuit of "professional artist" status.

By the time I was again working in my studio, my health had begun failing. For the next three years, I was well, working and playing hard for three or four months, then abruptly bedridden with a lingering illness that lasted for another three months. I repeated this cycle for three years before falling apart a final time in my early thirties.

Unable to work for five years, my plans and goals were moved up to the most unreachable shelves. Becoming healthy became my only goal. Along with this new plan came a growing realization, an insight which I traced back to my early twenties when I began sensing trouble in my approach to life.

I discovered that, for myself, the primary function of planning and goal setting was to provide a direction in which to focus my energy. Whether I reached my goal or not was secondary. I had unknowingly put my whole attention on becoming a psychologist, a writer, an actor, a sculptor while losing sight of the main ingredient of accomplishing anything: the process.

Since that first spark of realization, I have broadened my approach. Today I look first at the process to decide if I want to become involved. If the process itself is not enough reward, then I seriously question the benefit of immersing myself in work with which I am not in harmony.

Take a look at your life. Are you in harmony with your work, with your sense of self? Or are you still a prisoner of the "Dream" of becoming a "Something?" For me, being focused on what I am doing is better than keeping an eye on what I am trying to become.

25

TAKING RISKS

THE MIDDLE PATH

"How can that be?" you ask. "How can taking risks be anything but an extreme?"

Do even the most conservative people lead risk-free lives? Is getting married a risk? Is crossing the street a risk? Without realizing we are doing so, all of us take many risks each day. To live risk-free is to be dead.

Risk is different from danger. To put ourselves in danger consistently is choosing extremes. Risk involves thought and guidance. Reckless living puts us in peril.

On one extreme, we have danger and peril, while the other extreme holds death and decay. Down the middle of this road of life runs risk-taking.

We can be smart about the risks we take. One friend of mine felt so hurt in a relationship a few years ago that he became extremely reluctant to risk his heart again in a new love affair. He went to work and came home and did not do much else. What is that person missing? Life. As far as I know, he is still repeating his pattern, which is his choice to make.

Another friend has thrown herself into new relationships over and over again. Yes, she goes through pain, and yes, she is learning to be smarter about her choices of partners, but she is living life on her terms, taking risks.

How and when we take our risks is important. Learning from the risks we have taken is more important. If we want to live life fully, being willing to take risks is very important.

Take an inventory of the meaningful choices you have made in the past year. Have you often put yourself at risk? More than a few times? At all? How have your risks turned out? How did you grow from the risks you took? What could you do smarter next time?

If you had a bad experience in your love life, did you let your emotional needs lead you into another situation too deeply and too quickly? Perhaps you did just the opposite. Maybe you did not want to face your buried fears and hurts, so you refused to open up enough to keep any relationship growing.

The same principles apply to our work lives, relationships with children, extended family, and friends; almost everything we do and everyone we meet. Did you risk rejection and smile at the stranger on the street? Or did you miss the moment, which could have boosted your day and the day of another person? Did you risk feeling like a fool by standing up to ask a question in the seminar you took last month? Probably no one else would think you were foolish, but even if someone did, so what?

Taking risks does not mean putting ourselves in danger. For me, not taking risks is a danger—the peril of encouraging decay. I do take smarter risks now than I did ten, twenty, and forty years ago, but not all my risks are smart. I make a mess periodically. If I do not go over the edge once in a while, I wonder if I have lost touch with where the edge is.

Find your own rhythm, find what works for you by risking wisely, and you will increase your risk of living a happy life.

26

WANT A BETTER JOB?

YOU MAY NEED TWO FOR A WHILE

A re you trying to figure out what you "really want" to do with your life? I often met clients in financial trouble in my mortgage business because they changed their employment without thoughtful planning. Some of these people suffered an injury at work or had their companies lay them off, which are difficult to anticipate circumstances. More people, though, left jobs because they focused primarily on what they wanted instead of planning the best way to make an employment change.

My clients seem to have the most difficulty shifting from paycheck employment to self-employment. Many people accustomed to living on a paycheck are not prepared for the additional demands on a self-employed person. Doing the work which earns the income is only a part of the work needed to run the new business.

One client I interviewed had been employed for twenty years as a sheet metal worker. He felt he knew everything there was to know about his business. He had accumulated the needed skills and tools over the years.

Three months before I met him, he had quit his job and opened his own business. He had not starved, but business was not flowing in as he had hoped. His van needed replacing, and he was behind in his mortgage payments. He was also at a loss as to how to effectively manage the paperwork required in his business.

This client was skilled in his profession but unprepared to be a businessman. If he had taken business management and computer classes, created a reserve fund by taking out a loan on his home, and bought a newer van before he quit his regular job, he would have had a much better chance of succeeding.

Another client was floundering in his job as a painter because his employer did not provide steady work. We worked on a marketing plan for him. He stayed in his old job long enough to acquire the office equipment he needed. Six months later, this painter had more work than he could manage and handled his self-employment well, even though running his business required more non-productive time than he had anticipated.

The sheet metal worker had done sporadic free-lance work on the side for several years before he left the security of his paycheck. Had he increased his self-employment workload while keeping his paycheck job for a several-month transition period, he would have improved his chances of staying out of financial trouble. Often to create a new job for ourselves, we need to work two full-time jobs for a while.

Each of these clients was willing to take risks in their lives. Some were more successful than others and had less stress in their lives. But each person put themselves on the line, staking their financial freedom on their ability to make their plan work. They all learned a lot about planning, working, and risk-taking.

To shift from one paycheck job to another in your field may not require working two jobs if you have a new position already lined up. But often people do not find the new job they want while still at their old job. If someone moves from one paycheck industry to another, they may start at a lower position in their new job.

So how can you go about creating a new and better job for yourself?

First, take a thorough look at your current job. Make a list of the things you do and do not like about your work. How many of the "do likes" are you likely to find in a new job? How many of the "do not likes" are things you can either adapt to with a little work on yourself or are negotiable?

Think through the major aspects of your job, then sit down with your employer. Be as positive and flexible as you can in discussing the elements of your job that you like, how you can strengthen yourself to do your job better, and better adapt yourself to the uncomfortable parts. By showing your supervisor that you are both thinking about your job and trying hard to adapt to it, you will increase the opportunity for your boss to respond positively and perhaps adjust your work to better suit you.

If you draw a hard line in the sand and tell your boss, "Change this or I'm out of here," you may be out of there before you are ready. Almost certainly, you will not get what you want. Everybody likes to be treated with care and respect. People like people who are willing to change and able to meet a situation half-way.

If your job will not work for you, and you are not ready to leap into self-employment, you still need to prepare for your transition. Your preparation may involve taking classes, working a second job to gain skills, seeing a career counselor, or talking to friends. The only constant is that you need to continue to support yourself and your family, if you have one, during your period of exploring, planning, and preparation. Most people do not have the luxury of a high-income spouse, friend, or relative willing to bankroll such a move. Supporting yourself while you improve your life will also build your self-imagine.

What about if you are not working or do not know what you want to do? In both cases, doing almost anything constructive will help you. Most employers react more positively to someone who is already working and who makes an effort to seek new or additional employment. If you look hard enough, you will be able to find work. Look at any job as a stepping stone to the next one, as part of your continuing education.

My editor Kate shared her experience that work environments can become toxic. What then? Self-preservation takes over. As a man, I have not had to deal with sexual harassment as many women have. This form of discrimination is real. If you feel your oxygen supply is reaching the danger point in your job, bailing out may be your best option. Sexual harassment can create emotional trauma. Look for signs that you are not your normal self and seek out nurturing environments if you possible can. You may be in a very vulnerable state. Talk to other women. So many men are clueless about the effects we inflict on the women in our lives—myself included.

The rough times a sudden transition can create are more than worth it if our personal freedom is on the line. In this situation, adopt a crisis budget and full-time job search. The next job you take will hopefully help prepare you for more fulfilling employment.

Being active and being around other people is an excellent way to clear out cobwebs and freshen your perspective. If you already mix regularly with a lot of people, try some new organizations or activities. Wherever you go, ask people questions about their work and experiences. Someone sitting next to you at the coffee shop may be working in what will become your new line of work. A casual conversation may lead you to a better job.

You can create a better job for yourself. Taking the time and making an effort to prepare yourself will help you choose better risks and smooth your transition as much as possible.

27

EAR HAIRS

GROOMING COMMUNICATES

This chapter is for men. Women amaze me with how many different looks they have. How a woman decides what to wear to look a certain way is a mystery to me.

If you are a man, pay attention. Would you wear a suit and tie to play golf? Probably not. Would you wear a suit and tie to court if you were on trial? Probably yes.

Perhaps you care little about what you look like because you are not concerned with what people think. Rising above public opinion can be freeing if you do not sabotage yourself.

Do you like to criticize the way others look? Be careful; some people put other people down trying to build themselves up. This approach will create new problems without accomplishing anything.

No matter what we think about ourselves, how we

look communicates something about us. Much of the quality of our lives depends on what we communicate. Communicate to your employer how much you dislike him, and you will be out of a job before finding another one. Fail to communicate to your sweetheart how much you love her, and your relationship will suffer.

Rock singers and accountants do not dress the same. If either dressed like the other when looking for work, both would be less likely to be hired.

Grooming cannot replace substance, but it can hide it. You are what you are, but dress in a black garbage sack, and few people will see the real you. What you are communicating is essential in your life. Taking care with your grooming can smooth rough passages and speed your ascent up whatever ladder you are climbing.

When the hair on top of my head went south, unknown to me, much of it landed in my ears. Hairy clumps sprouted in all the wrong places. Jane, my girlfriend of long ago, broke the news to me. We had been intimate for two weekends. On Sunday morning, Jane snuggled against me and said, "Mind if I trim your ear hair?"

"Ear hair? What ear hair?" I reached up to my left ear. "Oh. That hair." I played with the fuzzy stuff for a minute, then said, "Sure if you want to." I can imagine Jane holding her breath, wondering what she would do if I refused.

When Jane and I broke up, I moved to Hawaii. Too shy to ask a new barber to trim my ears, I struggled alone. Old Caucasian men have hairy ears. I was not yet forty. Remembering my sister plucking her eyebrows, I got my pliers. I ripped out a hairy clump and gasped at how much it hurt. Next, I tried shaving my ears—another mistake. I wore band-aids for two days.

In a little catalog that came in the mail, I saw advertised a small instrument for trimming nose hairs. I ordered it. By the time the device arrived, my ears were noticeably overgrown. The little trimmer was made of stainless steel and looked efficient. Luckily I did not then have a problem with hair in my nose, but since the trimmer was designed for that purpose, I decided to test it before pushing its design envelope.

Standing in front of the bathroom mirror, I put the trimmer into one nostril like an inhaler. I pushed the lever, spinning the cutting cylinder inside its housing. The trimmer jammed, and pain stabbed into my nose. As I jumped, the steel housing jerked from my hand, causing more pain. For a moment, I watched in the mirror as this grooming aid from hell swung wildly under my nose. Looking in the mirror complicated my reflexes, but I finally grabbed the little devil and ripped it out. Tears came to my eyes. I must have a low pain tolerance.

I tore apart the trimmer. The design was good, but the blade was very dull. Not about to put it near my ears, I threw it away.

My solution to unwanted ear hairs? I conquered my shyness about asking for a trim. With much less hair on top, requesting the extra work was easy to rationalize.

Paying attention to your ear hair, or whatever

element of your appearance is not communicating the real you, can open your pathway through both your professional and personal lives.

28

NETWORKING

PUTTING OUT YOUR MESSAGE

Perhaps you, like me, have some shyness. Nobody likes rejection, though many people have learned to sidestep it. Some of us are "people persons," some of us prefer to be by ourselves. Each of us has our own strengths and weaknesses, but to paraphrase one religion's teaching, "Spirit helps those who help themselves." When setting out to help ourselves, we usually run headlong into one of our weaknesses. The best way I know to grow past a weakness is to challenge it.

In the mortgage business, a loan officer has to know a multiple loan programs, how different loan committees analyze income, credit, property values, and how best to meet each borrower's goals. A loan officer needs to communicate with people on the business's technical side and with the borrowers who know little of the business.

All of these skills, though, are useless unless a loan officer has clients. How does he or she find clients? By marketing. Without marketing skills, a loan officer is not a loan officer. No matter how marketing is approached, the fundamental ingredient to finding clients is talking to people.

When some loan officers meet with clients, they focus only on the business at hand: pre-qualifying the client, taking the application, assembling the needed documents, shepherding the loan file through approval, and being with the borrower at closing. The last step for many loan officers is to be paid. Their next step is to begin looking for a new client.

What have these loan officers missed? They have failed to enable their clients to do what almost all happy borrowers are eager to do: refer friends to the loan officer who helped them meet their goal. If the loan officer lets his borrowers know during the loan process that he would appreciate them referring people to him after they close their loan, he will receive more referrals than just by assuming his wishes are known.

Why? The loan officer networked. He let someone know about his goals and was open to assistance. The principle of networking is just that simple: putting out your message.

How we network, where and with whom we network, what our message is about, and how we present it will, of course, affect how successful we become. The more we network, the better networker we become. The secret of networking is learning about other peoples' goals and helping them while making ourselves available for referrals.

Whether we are looking for more business, a better job, a date, a friend, an idea...no matter what we are seeking, networking can complement our other efforts to meet our goals.

29

DO COMMUNITY SERVICE

GIVING FREES US

Many of us go through periods of feeling we are stuck in a rut. The kind of rut does not matter. When I put my life on automatic—which I do periodically—I have reached a point where I can no longer live with myself unless I change my approach. Most of us go through cycles of activity and rest, which we can identify if we look closely into ourselves. Shifting from rest into activity can happen smoothly, can be a challenging and sudden transition, or may drag on uncomfortably for a long time.

To me, a rut is when my shift out of a rest phase into a period of dynamic living stalls. If you are struggling in a rut and cannot find the solution, consider doing some community service that is appropriate for you. Like any new adventure, you may need to try more than one option before finding what is right for your situation.

What good does community service do? Look

around you. There are people everywhere a little more lost than you. If you take the time and make an effort, you may make a difference in another's person's life. You may make a difference in your own life. You may or may not be aware of the effect of your actions, but sooner or later, you will feel the reward that comes from giving.

When I lived in San Francisco and was unable to earn a living, I was in a counseling program that required me to do some volunteer work. Before that time, I would help a friend without hesitation but did not consider taking time to do community service.

I spent eighteen months helping out at The Foundation for San Francisco's Architectural Heritage. The people at this nonprofit agency work hard to support San Francisco's efforts to retain its historic integrity. The staff was very appreciative of my office work. Being a part of their efforts helped me feel useful and productive. I also felt lighter by shifting my attention away from my health problems.

After my grandparents were gone, my father told me how he, his sister, and brother had made jokes every year when their parents disappeared for the day on their wedding anniversary. The kids presumed their parents were sneaking off to make whoopee. My father learned from a family friend that my grandparents had spent each anniversary day delivering baskets of food to the people in our small town who could not buy fully feed their families.

Giving frees us from self-involvement. Often when

we let go of a problem and relax our overly-concerned self, a solution pops up in a surprising way.

Not sure where to begin? Look in the phonebook, which means Google today for most of us. I found twenty-five listings in Yelp under "Best Volunteer Opportunities in Honolulu, Hawaii." However many you find in your area, reach out to one or more of them. A phone call and a visit will help you decide if a situation may be right for you and allow the agency to do the same.

If you choose to give through community service, your experience will be your own, unique to you and your situation. A constant that transcends individual differences is that giving provides a reward that cannot be duplicated any other way.

30

WANTING RICHES

IS THIS YOUR GOAL?

Does anyone not want a lot of money? Of the wealthy people, some are very bored with money, some want even more money, and some make a conscious effort to use their money to give to others. The great majority of the rest of us hunger for enough money to buy what we need or what we think we want.

What is this hunger really about? Hunger for money may be about desire. Most physical world desires require money to fulfill them, even the desire to help others with their physical needs.

The hunger for money may be about power. Power over others is the negative form of this hunger. The power to guide our lives is its positive form.

Hunger for power may also be about freedom. On the surface, the hunger may be for freedom from a repressive parent, boss, or political environment.

Deeper within ourselves freedom takes on a higher meaning.

Of the many forms of riches, the surface glitter that money buys is a trap. Once acquired, keeping material possessions requires more energy and can lead to obsession. The things of life are fine to have as long as we remain neutral about their being with us. An irony often plays out with people not finding the happiness they thought they would find in a nice car, bigger home, more jewelry, or finer clothes. Still feeling unfulfilled, they chase happiness even deeper into other things money can buy.

Often through losing our possessions, we discover the riches we seek cannot be found outside ourselves.

The happiness of the moment when something new comes into our lives is great but has no depth. The more someone is unhappy within themselves, the more likely they are to look for their happiness outside themselves. Emotional pain gets old fast. Most of us hit our limit and then look for ways to change how we feel. The quick ways to alter feelings—alcohol, drugs, escapist sex, power over others, anger, buying things—are easy to try. Later we find these paths are downward spirals, turning very difficult and destructive.

True happiness comes from within, from the investment of time and effort in making choices that help us grow. This happiness shows as a light within us, shining forth more vibrantly as we clear our inner overgrowth.

Money is a great tool and a lousy master. Let money

come into your life, be used wisely, and leave when it must without attachment. Work hard to grow and to be responsible for yourself and your family. Leave the things of life to Spirit, and you will attract riches of many kinds beyond your imagination.

31

WE PAY FOR EVERYTHING WE GET

AND GIVE

D o you think you can get something for nothing? Do you think the man who robs a bank and does not get caught pays no price for the money he takes?

On some level, most of us know we do not get anything for nothing, but many people do not live their lives by this principle. I am one of these people. I have been saying "No" to my finagling self for decades now, yet the impulses are still there.

About thirty years ago, I remembered repeatedly that I owed our mortgage company $170 for four megabytes of ram for my then-new computer. I had been paid three times since incurring the debt. Each time, I pushed what I owed to the company aside in my mind. Finally, I did see my behavior clearly and paid for what I received with my next paycheck. What was going on? I was finagling, avoiding my responsibility.

My level of awareness has expanded over the years about this part of myself. Clearly, I had more work to do then and still some now.

How much work you need to do in this area—and when you do it—is your concern about being aware of the debts you incur. Our awareness level does not change the principle of paying for what we get.

Not knowing does not excuse a debt. Ignorance of the law in our society does not relieve us of being responsible for our actions. This same principle applies to spiritual laws. There is no cop to arrest us, or court to answer to, for our spiritual debts in the physical world. Instead, we live our debts. Working to expand your awareness will enable you to better see how your actions are coming back to you.

When I first studied spiritual laws, I lived in San Francisco. One day Jane and I went to buy some earring- and necklace-making supplies. The woman who owned the supply house was rude, and her prices were high. When she put two items in my bag without ringing them up, I smiled to myself. "Serves her right," I whispered to Jane. I had saved four dollars.

Leaving the store, we walked under a raised freeway section on the way back to my car. A bird pooped on my shoulder. The cost to clean my jacket, $3.75 plus tax, was almost exactly the amount of money I had "saved" in the jewelry supply house. The incident nagged at me for a week until I made the connection.

A few years later I was talking on the phone to a different girlfriend. Suddenly she asked if I wanted to go to a movie. "When?" I said. "Now. I just remembered I have six movie coupons that cost four dollars each and they expire tonight. It's after 8:00 now, so we would have to go to a 10:00 show."

Too tired for a late movie I declined, but said, "Why don't you run over to the mall and surprise the last six people in line with free tickets. You would make them happy and avoid wasting your twenty-four bucks, too." My friend deflected my suggestion.

Ten minutes later, I again approached the subject by saying, "Imagine how happy we would be if someone gave us free tickets." My friend agreed but did not want to make the effort. She's missing such a wonderful opportunity, I thought, and soon said good-bye in a grumpy voice, my heart closing down.

I slept fitfully. The next morning, sitting quietly in contemplation, I realized that if giving away the tickets was so important to me, I should have done so myself. Maybe I am the one with an issue about giving, I thought.

An hour later, the phone rang. I listened to a young man tell me that if I signed up for one or more magazine subscriptions, 12.5% of the money would go to the Special Olympics. My "gift" to my friend the night before had just come back to me. I had a strong urge to send money to the charity to pay for the grief I had given my friend.

"I don't need the magazines," I told him, "but I can send you a check for $25, which would be the equivalent of $200 in magazine subscriptions." The dollar amount I chose without thinking about it.

The telemarketer was surprised but gladly gave me the charity's address. I wrote the check and mailed it that day. My cash flow was low. Since I was not sure when I would be paid next, $25 was more than usual to me.

Later, another friend pointed out with a grin that interest had already begun to accrue on my debt. The tickets in question had cost $24. A day later, my bill was up to $25. Grateful for both the awareness and to pay my debt quickly, I called my girlfriend and apologized for being grumpy and judging her. We laughed at my expense.

We pay for what we get and give, including if, like me, we give grief. Pay attention to what you want and what you do to get it. The more aware we are about what is happening, the more able we are to guide ourselves in an uplifting direction

32

APPETITE AND HUNGER

WHAT'S THE DIFFERENCE?

When I first started having serious health problems in 1980, I relied on traditional western medicine to prop me up. I had developed mild hepatitis symptoms. The infection was too mild to show up on blood tests but was still capable of leveling me for three months at a time. These episodes happened during periods of over-work and too much drinking. I would develop a viral throat infection and go to the doctor, who would give me antibiotics. The infection would pass, but I would be weak and too sick to work for another eight to ten weeks. In about three months, I would start the cycle again.

At the end of these three years, I finally admitted to myself I needed to make some changes in my life. I was still years away from realizing I had to take responsibility for my health, but my admission was a start.

Reading through different books at the health food store, I began buying vitamins and supplements. The more I read, the more it became clear that what I was eating was making getting healthy more difficult.

Being used to mid-western cafeteria food, New York-style Italian dinners, and drinking wine almost daily, I found changing my diet was not easy. My idea of dessert was a six-pack of dark beer and a family-size chocolate bar.

I ate different foods, read more about people who had changed their lives by eating smarter, made more changes in my diet, and gradually became used to eating much simpler foods. One guideline I learned was to eat whole food as much as possible. The more processed and the more ingredients on the label, the more potential a food had to cause complications I wanted to avoid.

My taste buds went through shock. Motivated by a deepening frustration with my declining health, I lost my attachment for "pleasure eating" and tried raw foods, vegetable juices, and fasting. As my body cleansed itself, I found I liked this new way of eating.

During this several-year-long process, I discovered my body gave me two sets of signals when it wanted food. What I had always called hunger, I learned, was often just appetite. The difference? For me, desire fuels appetite. My body's need for nourishment produces hunger.

Appetite and hunger: I contemplated this realization for months. Slowly I saw the way my body expressed itself as a metaphor for life. Desires work like appetite. The more I indulge my desires, the more power I give them, whether the arena is food, anger, or titillation. Most desires can lead to destruction if carried to the extreme. True hunger, though, is our higher self calling for nourishment. To grow, we must give ourselves high-quality nutrients of all kinds.

I found that if I had a craving and paused for a minute imagining myself eating that food, I could feel its effects inside me and know if it was a healthy choice or not. Like any meaningful inner guidance, I ignored it often. Gradually I learned to respect the effect of going against my body's messages and improved my choices. Awareness came before constructive action.

Experiment if you are curious. What will you feel after you eat that piece of cake you are lusting after? How will a fresh salad feel in your stomach instead of the burger and fries you are thinking about? Imagine drinking a large cola. Will you get jittery not long after? How differently would you feel if you drank a glass of water instead?

See if you can learn to discriminate between your appetite and your hunger, between your desires and your higher self's urge to nourish yourself. The more self-awareness you develop, the more opportunity you will create to guide yourself in a positive direction.

33

WHO IS IN CHARGE?

TRYING TO CONTROL YOUR WORLD?

Pain is usually behind our efforts to control our world. Most of us learn so many ways to hide, avoid, and not deal with what hurts us that we often become experts at creating smokescreens. Control is one smokescreen.

Some people go through a devastating romance and attempt to avoid more pain of this nature by controlling their emotions. Other people try to control the actions of those near them, so their weaknesses will not be challenged.

I spent much of my twenties trying to structure my world so that I would not hurt. The effort backfired considerably, causing my thirties to be focused on recovering from my twenties.

My pattern showed itself dramatically with my first girlfriend in high school, though I did not see it then. Andi and I went steady for six months from the spring of my junior year to the fall of my senior. We had a lot of fun exploring our passions and curiosities about life.

Coming to school one morning in the fall, Dwight, an annoying classmate, told me in the hallway that Andi had a new boyfriend. The last thing I wanted to hear coming from the last person I wanted to hear it from. It set me off.

In second period I wrote a long letter to Andi breaking up with her. I needed to stay in control. After school, I went by her house. She told me she had been on a date with an older boy that weekend. She was kind, a little scared, and told me how sorry she was.

I threw my folded letter at her, ran off her porch, jumped into Dad's Mustang, and burnt rubber for a block. Anyone who has driven a 1964 Mustang stick knows burning rubber is as easy as burning gas.

Andi later told me her mother watched me drive away, saying what a fool I was. She was not wrong. But I told myself I had broken up with Andi. I stayed in control!

Years later, while recovering from a pattern of foolish choices, I was given a spiritual principle, which has proven true, though not easy to follow.

"To ask others to adjust to my weakness will perpetuate my weaknesses. To adapt to what comes my way will help me grow stronger."

These words stopped me cold. I could not continue the way I was, embroiled in long, emotional discussions with friends and lovers about life and feelings, slowly twisting my viewpoints to avoid facing my fears.

I saw that I had been spending a tremendous amount of energy trying to take from life what I wanted while trying to reject the rest: a "cookie-cutter" approach.

Life is so much simpler for me when I watch what is coming to me to see what I need to learn. Doing the work is easier than avoiding it, and eventually, I have to learn it anyway.

Surrender your control to Spirit. Look both inward and outward to learn about the lesson you face today, knowing it will stay with you in some form until you master it.

34

LISTENING

AN ACT OF LOVE

How often have you told a friend about an experience, and they interrupted your story to say, "I've had that happen to me, too. It went like this..." Depending on how your friend handled themselves, you might feel validated or cheated. Why?

Most of us carry the need to be listened to by someone. The greater our need to be listened to, the more likely we will be a poor listener.

A peer counseling network I was once involved with taught that we are not allowed to cry through our pain from birth, which would allow us to release the hurt. Instinctively parents pick up their babies to comfort them when the little ones cry.

Some people can handle a baby crying longer than others, but eventually, almost everyone will try to quiet their child before the child is ready to stop crying. This premature end to expressing a hurt can create a small cobweb of clutter in our emotional selves. Growing up, we accumulate a large amount of this webbing, complicating our emotional responses.

One aspect of this emotional clutter is unprocessed anger. The child within us may still be upset. We were not allowed or encouraged to get rid of our hurts. One result of this accumulated, unresolved anger is the strong need to be listened to. This need sets a much different tone in a relationship than the one people share with each other when they have largely dealt with their anger.

During an eight-week training class of this peer counseling group, we paired off and took turns listening to the other person talk. In turn, we each experienced the difference in talking to someone who has agreed to be there with us for fifteen or thirty minutes. The talkers would then become listeners for an equal length of time.

Quickly the person in the talker role was able to open themselves to some of their buried pain, which they could then talk, cry, laugh, or scream about as much as they wanted. In class, we were shown how to be an effective listener and gently assist the talker in processing and hopefully discharging some of their old pain.

There was a contractual agreement within the group to not have any social contact with the group members, except to get together for counseling sessions. This group guideline helped to establish mutual trust and safety. I found this to be both uplifting and challenging, as I was deep in the throes of habitually hooking onto others to seek relief from pain.

Short of joining a similar peer counseling group, how can you become a better listener?

First, try listening. You may struggle to listen well, but keep trying. Sometimes I use the image of stapling my lips together. Sometimes I am too full of my own experiences and am not a good listener.

During this time, good friends of mine shared with me that they set a timer when they get home from work. Each person had five minutes to talk about their jobs. After those ten minutes passed, they agreed to put their work lives behind them for the rest of the evening or weekend. If one partner had an unusually stressful day, they could ask for extra time. The other person could give it or not, depending on their state of mind and heart.

After becoming a better listener, open yourself to having someone listen to you. You may know this special person and they may be listening to you much better than you listen to them. Or this person may have yet to come into your life.

By working to become the best listener you can be, you will attract good listeners. Sharing with a balance of talking and listening creates a more harmonious exchange and will help you live a more fulfilling life!

35

ACTIONS AND FEELINGS

ONE CREATES THE OTHER

I fell in love when I was seventeen. Life suddenly became golden. My feelings were new and wondrous to me. Six months later, we broke up. I was devastated and reacted angrily.

Most of us experience love and heartache. How we handle these feelings, how we handle all our feelings, can have a noticeable effect on our lives.

For years I hungered for the feeling I had with my high school sweetheart. Over the next thirty years, I was deeply in love with four more women. Each time brought the incredible high, which then slowly or quickly shifted into complications.

As I go through more experiences, I repeat many of my patterns. Sometimes I learn something. Slowly over the years, I grew aware of creating problems for myself by jumping so quickly into relationships with women. Almost all of my intimacies began suddenly.

By working with kind, skilled counselors and learning to sit quietly by myself contemplating a feeling, thought, or action, I learned how I run from pain. I have run to women, alcohol, drugs, sex, work...whatever helped me feel better in the moment. Afterward, I would feel worse about myself, which just became something else to run from.

For many years I did not see the repercussions from my dashes to supposed freedom. When I did begin to see the effects of my causes, I often ignored them. No matter how illusionary the freedom was, I had grown used to escaping into it. These destructive habits changed what I was feeling for a short time, but gradually I dug a deeper and deeper hole for myself.

In San Francisco, when I became ill again, I went to a good physician whose house I had been repairing. He examined me, ran blood tests and did not find any abnormalities. Then told me to see a psychiatrist.

I had learned nothing meaningful from doctors for several years, but no one had been this blunt with me. I had a strong inner knowledge that my body was struggling with something, but I took this man's advice.

I was very fortunate to find a therapist with whom I could work comfortably. Christine was kind, gentle, and clear about what I was doing to myself. I listened to her, but I resisted accepting a connection between my emotions and my physical health for months and months. I did, though, see the wisdom in what I discovered by talking to her.

Christine was an expert at helping me find my

solutions. She occasionally presented a viewpoint with just the right timing for my headstrong personality. Had she just told me what she thought I should do, our therapeutic relationship would have been unsuccessful.

I worked with Christine for four years. During this period, I spent time in the hospital, in a crisis center, a half-way house, and co-op housing for people trying to put their lives back together.

These years were not easy, for I had hung on to my destructive patterns for years. I was given warnings to change and opportunities to stop my downward spiral, which would have made the trip back up less harsh. I am grateful I finally listened when I did.

During the first two years of working with Christine—and other counselors who were a part of each care environment I stayed in—I made a conscious effort to stop the various ways I was hurting myself. I ate better, dressed warmly, stayed out of bars, stopped running after women, and tried hard to stay with the surging discomfort I felt in my solar plexus. This is where I store pain and anxiety in my physical body, and it is from this constant discomfort that I seek escape.

Underneath my fear of pain was fear. I learned I was giving this fear power over me by holding on to it. After this realization, I spent a month confused because I had presumed since I was now aware of what I was doing, I should be able to stop it. Other people may be able to " stop it," but I could not.

Gradually I realized life was more complicated than simply changing trains. The momentum of the train I wanted to leave was still with me: Karma was working off slowly.

After two years of doing everything I possibly could to help myself moment to moment, I experienced a good feeling about myself bubbling up inside. This good feeling was the first I could remember and took me by surprise. I was trying to survive. I did not know there was a reward coming.

This experience of feeling spontaneously good brought into focus a principle that I had been reading about and that Christine had mentioned casually.

The principle is "We create our feelings by the actions and thoughts we choose."

When this principle sunk in, I felt lifetimes lighter. No longer was I chained to my emotions. I could change how I felt, really change it for the better.

I would be delighted to share with you that life since then has been a steady climb upwards, each step getting easier and happier—but it has not. I slugged through my destructive patterns for years after, as I slowly shed them.

In a larger sense life does get freer and lighter with each constructive step I take. I have learned to love myself. Sometimes I regress. And sometimes, I can still love myself when I have chosen unwisely.

However we glide or stumble along our path, our experiences can be smoother with the awareness that we are creating our feelings of the next moment, the next day, the next years of our life by what we are choosing today.

36

EXPRESSING FEELINGS AND LOVE

FINDING BALANCE

My girlfriend of thirty years ago came from a different culture than mine. We shared rocky times together, struggling to find our balance, both as individuals and as a couple.

When we first met, she was very reluctant to open herself emotionally. She had been taught from birth that harmony in society was more important than any individual's feelings.

When my parents broke up before I was two, I went to live with my father's parents. My way to get love was to be as open as possible. Much later, a counselor at the hospital in San Francisco told me I had never developed a personal border. She used the image of an amoeba, whose porous membrane lets in nutrients and pushes out waste. Toxins are out. Good stuff is kept in. Because of my toddler's hunger for love, which I carried into my adult years, I took in everything, nutrients and toxins alike.

My girlfriend and I began our relationship from opposite directions. I was very clear that she needed to open up, but hazy at first about my lesson, which was to be more discriminating about what I give out and let in.

Many uproars later, we developed a deeper respect for each other and peace between us. I learned to give her space and to keep some for myself. Better able to contain my feelings, I became happier when alone, yet able to share with her without making myself unnecessarily self-protected. She discovered the wonders of really opening to another person and began learning about her personal limits.

So how does this affect you? Many American couples are the opposite of what my girlfriend and I were. The man is perhaps too closed, and the woman sometimes too open.

For a strong and clear relationship to develop, each partner must do their personal homework and take responsibility for themselves. Yes, couples often divide their work according to who does what best. Nothing is wrong with this approach unless it prevents one or both partners from growing.

Romantic involvement heightens our vulnerability, more readily highlighting our areas that need work. The same dynamics apply to all our relations, with different elements brought to the forefront.

Friendships are formed from shared interests, but the sharing is not always balanced. We do not see the imbalances as readily because we are not as vulnerable. If we have a strong argument with a good friend that does not get resolved, we usually will feel our life has gone out of whack. Not as intense as lovers' quarrel, but impactful just the same.

I used to be very skilled at finding a woman's weakness and supporting her in that area. The problems began when I used my giving as a bargaining tool to get what I wanted. Being in a relationship out of need, to pull from each other what we lack, can easily become a downward spiral.

When each partner works on strengthening themselves emotionally, physically, and spiritually, they gradually become able to be in the relationship to share, instead of getting needs met—the stronger and clearer the individuals, the healthier and more vibrant the relationship.

What can each of us do to balance the way we express our love and feelings? Look at ourselves in our current relationship. What behavior stands out? By working on these problem areas within ourselves, we will strengthen all our relationships

.

37

FINDING A LOVER

DO NOT LOOK!

Having lived about twenty five years of my adult life single and being a love-hungry, overly-giving male with an addictive nature, I spent a tremendous amount of energy pursuing women.

When not involved in a relationship, I seem to be caught in a hormonal jet stream, running from one flirtation to another. Since I have a great imagination, many of my encounters happened without the women even knowing I was interested.

In my twenties, I was a roman candle. In my thirties, severely depleted from how I acted in my twenties, I had to be more subtle. In my forties, I had moments of wild behavior, followed by weeks of recuperation, slowly morphing into an extended period of "What's the fuss?" My neutrality ended when I could not contain my yearnings, and I skulked through

Honolulu's nightlife for two or three hours, beginning my cycle anew.

What have I learned through all this? In addition to lessons like not pitting my will against Spirit's and that love grows from the inside out, I have learned countless times the best way to find a lover is to not look.

If you would like some meaningful company in your life, do things that interest you. Volunteer for a nonprofit organization, join a club, take hikes, work with yourself to be happier alone, accept your Karma whatever it may be, surrender to Spirit, go with the flow, change your feelings by more carefully choosing your actions—anything other than looking for a companion.

When I am anxious, mentally or physically, I go hunting. Women sense this and move out of the way. I feel like I am a wound-up toy soldier parading around with my little rifle, trying to find a shooting range.

This experience is humbling. I must need a lot of humbling.

If you are the hunting type, try letting your passions dissipate. Try letting someone find you attractive for a change instead of always being the predator. If you are not a hunter, guard against becoming passive and stay active.

In my twenties, I was free of common sense. Mellowing with age has been helpful, tempering my urges somewhat. Getting older and getting sick probably saved my life. Getting married at age fifty changed my life completely, for the better. Working to strengthen our marriage accomplished even more.

If you find yourself compulsively hunting for a lover, try your best to divert your energy. Loneliness is our higher self's hunger for unconditional spiritual love.

We find spiritual love by giving unconditionally. Looking for a lover is not unconditional giving. Learning to love ourselves will help us open to this love of Spirit. As we open, we radiate this love, touching others around us. We become more able to feel love, give love, and are far more attractive to others.

At times I do not receive love from others gracefully. When I am hungry for love, I am willing to accept what I am hungering for—illusion or not—but often, I reject love when someone is giving me love in a way that does not match my hunger. Opening ourselves to receive is important. Being humble enough to accept what is given is equally important.

Once we learn to open ourselves to Divine Love, Spirit just may bring someone into our lives. Until we are ready both inside and outside for a relationship, looking usually will not help us find someone uplifting to share our life.

38

HANDLE YOUR ANGER

IT WILL COME BACK TO YOU

D o you get angry? What do you say to yourself afterward? Whether you get angry at yourself for having gotten angry, dismiss your anger as part of life, or stop and take responsibility for your actions—it is human nature to try to justify ourselves.

What does it mean to you to justify an action? Most people would say, "To justify is to say, 'It's OK.' It was OK for me to be angry with Sarah. She was an hour late picking me up." Hard to argue with being angry at someone who makes us wait for an hour. Or is it?

What does anger accomplish? Does anger bring people closer together? Will anger get the project finished more quickly? When you get angry in traffic, does your commute then smooth out? No, anger does not accomplish anything. Anger destroys.

"But getting angry makes me feel better," some

people say, or "I let off steam when I get angry." Sure we can vent frustrations by getting angry, but with what result? We may feel better in the moment, but then we have the effects of our anger to deal with. Anger does not dissipate like steam. Anger lingers in our hearts and in the hearts of those with whom we have shared our anger.

To justify anything we do is an attempt to neutralize the effects of our actions. Do you believe you can undo what you have done? I do not believe I can change the effects of the cause I have set in motion. I can change what I do, but not what I have done.

I worked closely with an attorney during my mortgage business years. He had helped several of my clients solve sticky problems. When he needs a mortgage, though, Steve is not my client. He turns to Bob, my senior partner.

Two months after applying with Bob to refinance his home, Steve was getting panicky. He was buying out his roommate and wanted the timing to go smoothly.

During a phone conversation with Steve about a mutual client, he let me know how upset he was that his loan had not yet closed. I had heard two people in the office mention how anxious Steve was getting over his loan, so I was not surprised he was irritated. I was surprised that he became hostile and angry when I mentioned that he might be overreacting.

Up to this point, I was breaking even. Steve is a business friend and a professional in the business world who handles judges, other attorneys, clients, and his

staff with seeming ease. When Steve began blaming our
company for his problems, I got angry. I did not need to
get angry. I was not part of Steve's transaction with our
company, but I dug in my heels anyway and became as
obstinate as was he. We threatened to stop doing
business together but ended our conversation before
doing irreparable damage.

What did I accomplish? My anger lingered with me
for several days, gnawing at my serenity. Bob closed the
loan with Steve and gave him the best of deals, making
Steve happy. I felt foolish after the loan closed, still
living with my lingering bad feelings. The office had
moved past the crisis, but I had not. Getting embroiled
when I was not a part of the transaction: How stupid
could I be?

I do have some strengths in the business world, but
when it comes to diffusing anger, I am grateful Bob is
good at it. At best, I stumble through tense times, happy
if I do not make matters worse. Steve and I did later
make our peace. I apologized for my role in our
unpleasant conversation, and he acknowledged how
vulnerable and anxious he had been feeling.

Did I pay for my anger? Yes, I paid for it by feeling
lousy about myself for days. Perhaps I paid for my
actions in full, or I may have more yet to pay. I will
control my temper better for a while...until the next
time I lose it.

We are continually pulled between the positive and
negative energies here on earth. Sometimes we get
angry.

When you get angry, take a moment as soon as you can and admit to yourself that you have just created some destructive energy that will come back to you. You may not know what you have set in motion, so just acknowledge your actions and the possible results. Blaming yourself will not help. Just accept the responsibility.

We may not be aware of the energy when it does come back to us. When we have unpleasant things happen, most of us are mystified. Where did that come from? I did not see that coming! I do not need that in my life!

Our energy does come back to beat us, trip us, and humiliate us—it also comes back to please us, soothe us, and make us feel loved. Whatever we put out comes back.

If we keep an awareness that our energy will return, we probably will be less tempted to get angry.

39

OPINIONS

ARE YOU HANDCUFFING YOURSELF?

D o you have opinions? Most of us do. Do you have opinions of people, events, or things you do not care about? Most of our opinions concern something we care about, perhaps passionately.

If we dig deeper, we probably will find our cares, passions, and desires are at the root of our opinions. If we do not care about something, and if this something does not stimulate any other emotional response in us, then why waste the energy to have an opinion? Most of us do not.

What does an opinion do? An opinion draws a line in the sand. The line may be casually drawn and easily erased, or it may be a deep trench. Which kind of opinions do we hold most often? Why? How important are your opinions to you?

Opinions can be a substitute for knowledge,

especially when we feel insecure. Ever been in a heated discussion that took you into an area you knew little about? Perhaps you reached the point where you were defending a position you were not sure of. Many of us surround ourselves with opinions rather than admit we do not know as much as we would like to know.

Opinions can be an attempt to control others. Look what Hitler did with his opinions. We use opinions in many different ways. Why?

On some level, my opinions make me feel good. My opinion is that I am like most people in this sense. You have read a lot of my opinions in this book so far, along with insights coming from experiences.

Opinions are shadows. Awareness is the light. Opinions have a relationship to awareness, similar to how beliefs relate to experience. You may believe you can run a four-minute mile, graduate from college, or find a better job. When you do any of these things, then you know you can; you have experienced it. If you train hard and your best mile is run in 5:50, then it may be time to revise your belief based on your experience— that you cannot run a four-minute mile.

In the same way, opinions can be stepping stones to awareness. If we hold tightly to our opinions, though, we can prevent ourselves from taking the next step. The person who believes people of a different ethnic background are inferior to themselves may never learn the truth. Being open to learning gives us the flexibility to change an opinion—or let it go altogether.

Opinions, like beliefs, can keep us closed. One key

to whether we learn or stagnate is how we hold our opinions. Held lightly with an inquiring and open attitude, we can change our opinions as quickly as we reach a new awareness. Clutched to our breast in defiance, however, opinions will hold us down like an anchor. The heavier the anchor, the farther we sink.

Is it possible to be opinion-free? Yes, I think so. Clearly, I have yet to reach this level. Opinions cause problems in my life. As I learn to be more neutral about things and use my energy more wisely, I find more peace.

Deeply involved in writing this book of opinions—it could be titled Unsolicited Advice From Nobody You Know—I find myself back-sliding. A friend called me during the first draft of this manuscript with a problem about selling her car. She had entrusted her ex-boyfriend to sell the car, but he had not gotten as much money for it as he had planned. I asked my friend a few questions and discovered her ex-boyfriend had bought the car from her prior to selling it, signed for the title, and made no provision to split the profit, if any. My friend was feeling torn, not sure what was right for her to do.

Immediately I saw what I thought was right for her to do and told her so. I completely missed the point. This was her experience. What was right for me may not be right for my friend. Whether my friend made the "right" choice or not, choosing for herself, acting on her choice, and then seeing the result of her actions in both the outer world and inside herself is more important than whether a "right" choice is made. Why? Because this is how we learn. Subconsciously my friend set up the car transaction to learn something. Maybe she felt better after I gave her my approval, but did that help her grow?

Opinions can easily cause more trouble than they are worth. Opinions about people can be the most troublesome. When carried to an extreme, these opinions can be destructive. In today's world, media bombards us with opinions and material from which to form opinions. In our environment, holding opinions is rarely questioned.

As uncomfortable as it may feel at first, try holding your opinions more lightly, voice them less often. Let these non-productive thoughts float away. Perhaps you will become opinion-free, and then you can email me to tell me how you accomplished this feat.

Hold opinions too tightly and we handcuff ourselves. Instead, recognize opinions as potentially bothersome fluff and give them little room in your life.

40

TOXINS

THEY ARE TRICKY

To celebrate Thanksgiving in 1972, I quit smoking. I had grown up watching my father smoke. I knocked the ash off his cigarette when it got too long and cleaned his ashtrays for him when they overflowed. When I was five, I ate burnt match heads until my grandmother made me stop. Smoking seemed natural to me.

In the fourth grade, I found a half-smoked cigarette my father left unfinished and shared it with my cousin behind the rose bushes on the secluded side of my grandparent's home. The cigarette tasted too hot and made us cough. We found thirty cents, went down to the gas station on Ninth Street where no one knew us, and bought a pack of Kools and some matches. We hurried back to the rose bushes and lit up. Kools were just as hot as the cigarette butt had been. Determined to smoke, we overcame our disappointment with the taste and finished the pack in two hours.

Neither my aunt nor my grandmother understood why we were so sick that night. I did not smoke again until I was sixteen. When I did start, I developed the same zest for excess I had on that fourth-grade afternoon. Within a year, I was smoking four packs a day of unfiltered Camels. Since I did not smoke at home or in school, I once calculated I smoked a cigarette every six minutes when I was free, loose, and not yet twenty-one.

After graduating from high school, I discovered Picayunes and Home Runs, reportedly made with wild Mexican tobacco. Whatever they contained, they were far stronger than the Camels and Lucky Strikes I had been smoking. I also got into pipes, cigarillos, and rolling my own. With all this smoking going on, plus inhaling moderate amounts of marijuana, I was seldom without something lit stuck in my mouth. Even when I had pleurisy at age eighteen, I only slowed my smoking rather than quit.

Two years after my bout with pleurisy, I got a little worried about my lungs. I switched to Springs, a "light" menthol cigarette, and cut back to two packs a day. My consciousness awakens slowly, but even I saw smoking was bad for my health, so I tapered off for several months. I reduced smoking to such a minimal nicotine intake that I got headaches and became nauseated when I smoked my first cigarette each day.

Happily, on that Thanksgiving day, I quit and have not looked back.

Clearly, smoking did not create good health for me. After quitting, I found I could no longer drink ice tea without feeling shaky and unable to sleep. This was curious since I had ice tea with meals for years, along with three packs of sugar per glass. My body felt more sensitive to food, too. Because I had stopped drinking tea for about a year before quitting smoking, I assumed that while I had cleansed my body of nicotine, I had also cleaned out some other not-so-good things. Since experiencing the unpleasantness of smoking when not used to the habit, I wondered if there were other things I was putting into my body that were not very healthy. Perhaps I was growing sensitive to their subtle destructiveness.

Ten years later, when I had to clean out my body in a more profound way, I again discovered a sensitivity to some foods and activities after eliminating them. Butter, fat, marijuana, cocaine, alcohol, rock music, coffee, grease: the list of foods and activities I could no longer handle after quitting them grew long.

From these experiences, I developed a theory: "Just because I do not feel bad when eating a certain food or doing a certain activity does not mean that the food or activity is good for me."

One way I found to test if something is good for me was to stop it for a while. I tested wheat and felt better if I avoided bread. When I ate bread again, I felt worse quickly. I tested Mexican food with mixed results. Corn was better than wheat for me, but I felt shaky if I ate too many chips. I found that over a period of time, my body changed in how it handled some foods and experiences. New Age music felt better to me than the rock music I had loved for years. The more I cleaned out, the better I felt, but the more sensitive I became to marginally unhealthy foods and activities.

Since then, I have become increasingly more aware of what is toxic for me. Take an inventory of your life. Experiment with anything you think might be subtly harmful to you, but understand that cleansing your body is a process with cycles of its own. You may feel worse at first, but patience will help you endure the discomfort that periods of both change and cleansing bring. The more toxins you eliminate from your life, the freer you will feel.

41

RATION TELEVISION

LIKE ANY HABIT-FORMING SUBSTANCE

In my experimenting to find what was healthy and what was not, I tested television. After not watching anything on the tube for a year, I found myself feeling shaky and unsettled after sitting down for an hour program. What I watched made a difference. Laugh tracks proved more unsettling than National Geographic.

A sensitive person by nature, I have grown more sensitive by pushing myself beyond reasonable limits. I know that I am sensitive to some things which are healthy for most people. Maybe, just maybe, I experience a not-so-healthy reaction to some things which are not healthy for most people, but they do not know it because they are too healthy to beware of a small drag on their bodies...yet.

Like a canary in a nerve gas manufacturing plant,

maybe people like me act as a warning siren of bad stuff approaching. Television is a good example.

What does television do to you? "Nothing," most people will say, and there is a lot of truth in that. Most television programs do offer a lot of nothing.

You cannot get any exercise sitting in front of a television. We do not communicate in a meaningful way while watching TV. Mental stimulation is limited by most programming. Almost everyone eats too much in front of the tube. So what do we get?

We get dull and fat. We become slugs with programmed emotions. Television programs and advertising depend on creating specific emotional responses in viewers to be successful. Do you want to be programmed by someone else?

The physiological environment we put ourselves into by sitting in front of a television is questionable. Where do all those electrons go, which bombard the inside of the cathode ray tube we look into? The electrons are aimed straight at us. Last summer, after years of no television in my home, I bought a VCR and monitor. When I watched a long movie—or if I sat too close to the TV—I felt a little nauseous and shaky inside, like I had been bombarded by countless electrons that had no business bombarding me. Flat-screen TVs probably have a lesser detrimental effect on us. Or maybe their negative effect has yet to be detected.

A therapist I worked with in San Francisco told me she limited her ten-year-old son to thirty minutes of television a night. Why? "Because," she said, "he becomes a maniac if he watches any more than half an hour of television."

If you are concerned about becoming a slug with programmed emotions, try not watching television for a week or a month, then watch an hour program. You may find you feel jangly inside, hungry for any snack, and compelled to watch more and more TV. If so, reduce your television to thirty minutes a night and have no fattening snacks. In time, you may find you seldom watch TV at all.

42

GIVING OTHERS FREEDOM

A SIGN OF SPIRITUAL STRENGTH

To me, there is no wrong way back home to God. We all walk our individual paths. We are guided by our choices in the moment, the momentum of all our past choices, the degree of attachment we hold to our passions, and, most importantly, how much we consciously work to open ourselves to Spirit. We create problems for ourselves when we say to another person, "This is the way," without adding, "...if it feels right to you." We stumble in this way just as easily whether we are embroiled in darker energies or have learned to bring a new level of light into our lives. The surest way to lose awareness is to force it upon another.

Giving Others Freedom is a spiritual law, just like gravity is a physical world law. Violate this spiritual law, and we imprison ourselves in the Karma we create until we work through it.

In 1988, I was in Los Angeles on business and called a friend. Ron and I had been close to in the early '70s. We had not seen each other in the intervening years. Our last two visits had been rocky, so as I took a cab from my hotel to his new home, I wondered what harmony remained.

Ron had insisted I go with him to his spiritual group meeting before we had dinner. My inner nudge had said his group was not for me, but I wanted to support him, so I agreed.

He was busy on the phone when I arrived at his home, and we left quickly. Between his home and the meeting, we had too little time and too much distraction to reconnect.

Once at his meeting, and too late to leave gracefully, I learned his spiritual group was the same religious sect of a former roommate of mine. My roommate had chanted daily to bring material things into her life, oblivious of the karmic implications of her actions.

I watched my friend lead the meeting and discovered he was the regional leader of this group. As he asked each person in the room about their recent experiences, I listened to their tales of wanting and sometimes receiving new cars, clothes, jewelry, furniture, stereos, and other material goods. The list was amazing. Twice he reminded the people at the meeting that their chanting's real goal was to bring them closer to God, but each time he said this in an off-handed way. No one else at the meeting mentioned anything but their new toys.

Two people who were new to the group were pressured about returning and becoming permanent members. Before the group started chanting, he asked me when I would be coming back. I said, "Never, as far I as I know. I have my own spiritual path."

He then told the group, "BC is an old friend of mine. I will handle him later." I wondered what the hell he meant.

During the chant, I sang a one-word sound, "HU," which is, for me, a love song to God. Singing this simple sound clears away my negative energy, helping me have a higher viewpoint. During the chant, a man sitting next to me kept pushing a sheet of paper in front of me with the group's chant written on it. I indicated to him I would not be participating. He kept pushing until I had to make myself very clear.

After the meeting, dinner with my friend was strained. Our old harmonies had faded, and I let him know his spiritual path was not for me. When we said good night, I felt angry at him for what he did and at myself for not saying what was in my heart.

This man, my one-time dear friend, did not give me the spiritual freedom to be who I was. He was not content to let me have the experiences I chose. Instead, he tried to push his path on me in the short time we were together.

Why do some people say their spiritual path is the only true one? Years ago, when I was new to my spiritual path, I wanted others—such as my girlfriend Jane—to join with me. Why? I felt unsure spiritually and wanted company to convince myself I was on the right path. I soon learned the spiritual law of Giving Others Freedom, but it has taken time and work to live it.

Attempting to pull people onto a spiritual path is a powerful weapon of darkness. Ironically choosing power over love is often done by a person who has seen some spiritual light. When we dash up the spiritual ladder, it is easy to get off balance and think we know what is best for someone else.

Holding a doorway open for anyone interested and letting them come and go as they choose can be a wonderful act of service. Pressuring someone to join anything is not giving freedom; it is attempting to take it away.

We each create and earn our experiences. Choose your experiences wisely and let others choose their experiences freely. Giving freedom increases our own.

43

MORALS

A POOR SUBSTITUTE FOR RESPONSIBILITY

I magine a world identical to ours here on Earth, but in this imaginary world, the effect of each thought, spoken word, and action are instantly clear to all involved. In this imaginary world, people would be billed on the spot for what they did. In some cases, they could choose a payment plan or deferred payment, but each person's daily baggage reflected the additional weight of even the smallest unpaid debt.

How do you think behavior in this imaginary world would differ from our own? Do you think people there would be more responsible than we are here on earth? I think people are more accountable when the illusion of "getting away with something" is lifted.

I grew up learning what I should not do by exceeding the limits set by my father, my aunt, grandparents, and teachers. The loss of love was my great motivator. In my teens, I learned our society judged a person's actions by a vague standard called "morals." Murder and spouse-swapping were instantly pronounced "immoral" by my grandmother. My father agreed that murder was not productive but was more forgiving toward the idea of sexual experimentation. I was confused.

As I met other people, I learned my father and grandmother were not the only ones to disagree about morals. Some cultures encourage what other cultures condemn. Reportedly an area of Tibet at that time allowed women to have more than one husband. In Indiana, that is immoral. In Hawaii, many cultures mix at odd angles. At least one group within a religion found in both Hawaii and on the mainland endorses polygamy.

In our American society, thievery is common, unfortunately. When I visited Bali in the early 1990s, I was told there was virtually no crime, even though the people there had few possessions and tourists brought through all kinds of goodies.

What is the difference? In America, many people focus on what they can get for themselves today with little or no understanding that we pay for everything we receive. No one is exempted from this principle. Balinese people grow up with an ingrained understanding of Karma. I asked Eravan, our Balinese driver, about crime in Bali. "Noooo," he said, smiling. He shook his head and laughed, "No one here make stealing. Why steal when is stealing from self? Only crime here is by people from Jakarta and some few foreigners. Bali very with peace."

Balinese people know that to harm another is an illusion: they would be harming themselves. They know their act of aggression comes back to them in a way Spirit chooses. The Balinese may not recognize exactly how Spirit asks them to pay for their violations of Karmic Law, but they have complete confidence the karmic debt will come due.

Karma is not unique to Bali. The expressions, "What goes around comes around," and "As you sow, so shall you reap," show the concept of Karma as a part of western culture, too.

The Balinese, and all people who consciously live their lives with an awareness of Karma, govern their actions by principles that go beyond morals. Morals are changing codes of behavior. Morals do have a purpose in a world where people rarely take full responsibility for their actions. Often though morals are used to control rather than educate.

In the imaginary world discussed earlier in this chapter, morals would not be necessary. Why attack someone when you know without question you can only lose? If someone else hits us, they have incurred a debt. Why should we then hit them back? If we are acting in self-defense to protect ourselves, our family, our country, our freedom, then the price we pay for our actions is lifted. Most aggression today, though, is motivated by a desire for power.

The small actions of life add up. Kindness clears our path; malice makes our lives harder.

For a week, assume you are fully accountable for everything you do. Relax while you live this experiment. Making mistakes is part of being human and one of the ways we mature as spiritual beings. Remember, no one is grading you. There is no arbitrary authority who will step in and pronounce you a bad person. Assume the Law of Karma is real. Assume as well that you are living with full awareness of this law and in harmony with the give and take of your choices. Remember your thoughts and spoken words count as much as your actions.

At the end of the week, look back on your behavior. Did you take a step up in awareness? Did you live life with more consciousness about how you affect the world you live in, how you create your world?

Learn to live in harmony with the spiritual Law of Karma—by any name you wish—and you will uplift your life.

44

WHO ARE WE?

SOUL!

When I was fourteen, I awoke one morning and realized I was not part of my father. Perhaps this is normal for teenagers, though none of my friends ever mentioned similar thoughts. Until that day, what my father thought, I thought. Dad's opinions about music, UFOs, reincarnation, other people's behavior were my opinions.

This was not a fun time in my life. I loved my father desperately. My parents split up just before I turned two. My mother traveled to California with my father's trombone player—without my sister and me—then was unable to come back for us. We went to live with Dad's parents. My father became an indulging uncle, stopping by our grandparents' Illinois home in mid-winter to visit us with fun toys and a Florida tan. By my early grade school, we spent our weekends and summers with Dad. At the beginning of high school—and just a few months before my realization—my sister and I moved in with him full-time.

My father was not an easy person to be around. His tempered flared quickly, and he seemed to be ensnared in one troublesome business situation after another. His neediness drove his love for my sister and me. I was delirious to be with him every day, happy to ignore the unpleasant side of life. For me then, it was no small discomfort to realize that I had made myself an appendage of him. I felt like I did not exist outside of my father.

A year after my realization and working to fill in the hollow core I felt inside, I further realized that I did not like my father very much. I loved him as desperately as ever but saw that he often was not nice to people. When he wanted something, he would be charming. When he got what he wanted, he no longer seemed to care about this or that "good friend." He talked about some of his friends from childhood lovingly, but they were never around.

In my thirties, when living in San Francisco, sick, unable to get well, and working with my therapist, Christine, she told me one day that my father, as I described him, was a "dry alcoholic." Dad stopped drinking in his mid-twenties I knew from family friends, so I had to think about what Christine meant. I decided that I did not know what a dry alcoholic was, but I did know loving my father was like hugging a fan. I felt some relief, but I got very cut up in the process.

Through experiences during my spiritual exercises, I have become aware of entering into this lifetime to repay certain debts and to learn some particular lessons before moving on to a higher level of service. The first debt I repaid was to my father. I have not always been graceful to him in past lives and needed to be of service toward him for some time. That period ended when he died.

My hardest lesson so far in this lifetime is learning, again and again, the difference between power and love. In the way my life and body formed, exercising power has not been an option for me, unlike some past lifetimes. I am grateful for this condition because I would have been even more beat up physically if I had outer power to flex.

What did I do early in high school during my year of soul-searching to learn about myself? At night I lingered in that inner world between being consciously awake and fully asleep. Some nights I never went to sleep. Though tired, I always found the energy to get through the next day. Hovering nightly in the inner worlds, I began to awaken the next morning with a knowingness about ways people or the world worked that I did not have the night before.

After a while, I called this "learning without doing." Slowly I began to feel more whole. The completion of this period for me came five years later when I became friends with a fellow who worked at the pizza place near our home. John was ten years older than me and had been in the Marines, been around the world, done things, and been with women in ways I could not yet fully dream about. Yet, in our conversations, we had a very similar worldview. John had developed his outlook from worldly experiences; I had gained mine from inner-worldly experiences.

All during this time of self-discovery, a question nagged at me: "Who am I?" When I was young and went to Sunday School with my grandparents, I was told I have a soul. I knew I had a mind and a body...and I accepted that I had a soul, but what or who was I? Nobody ever told me.

My doorway to the inner worlds closed when I neared my fifteenth birthday. Girls and cars became important to me. During my time of inner world awareness, I had a warm, secure feeling about myself, about who I was, but I never had the words to describe my true self. Twenty years later when the inner world doorways opened again, I found the words and discovered they had been with me all the time.

I do not have a soul. I am Soul. Changing one small modifying word cleared up who I am. I felt instantly at home with this personal refocus. I have a body, emotions, the karma of my past lives, both a conscious and a subconscious mind—but I am none of these. I am Soul!

The time I spent when I was fourteen cruising the inner worlds was a time spent with my higher self, with myself as Soul. My lower world bodies were left in my bedroom, no longer able to separate me from my true self.

How did I gain this awareness? Through being willing to take risks, through being fortunate to live now in a time of great freedom, through being hungry to know my true self, and through being given gifts I can only assume I have earned.

Follow your inner nudges. So often, they come from our higher selves. Follow your inner guidance to know yourself as Soul.

45

POSITIVE AND NEGATIVE

EARTH IS BOTH

Think life is hard? You are right. Ever wonder why life is so hard? It is because the physical world is the lowest of the lower worlds of Spirit.

We can choose to look at life here as hell on earth, which we can certainly create for ourselves, or as part of our spiritual training. Whether our present lifetime more closely resembles summer camp or boot camp, it reflects our past choices and current attitudes.

Above a certain level in the worlds of Spirit, above the dual polarity of the lower worlds, above time and space stretch the vast regions of the pure positive worlds of Spirit.

Below these higher regions of pure positive energy, life is subject to the push and pull between positive and negative energy. The farther down the spiritual world's ladder, the more hold the negative energy has on the Souls living there.

Living in the physical world is not a punishment. Greater opportunity for spiritual growth exists here than in the higher regions because of this pull between the positive and negative energies. How much have we learned during the periods of our life when things were smooth? As much as when we met resistance and had to struggle to take our next step?

If you are at all like me, you learn more when you have to work harder. This does not mean that suffering in itself will bring spiritual growth. Even when life here is hard, would you trade it for an easy time, an easy job, and a dimmer awareness?

Soul often reincarnates here on Earth after spending an in-between lifetime on one of the lower inner worlds just above the physical, learning about the meaning of its last physical world lifetime and preparing for its next venture into the physical. Soul can create the ability to choose its next lifetime based on what it has earned and is ready to work on next. As fascinating as our history is, history is only information unless the information is relevant to my—or your—specific spiritual needs to help us take our next steps.

The negative power is part of Spirit as much as the positive power. Both forces are our teachers. One of the traps of the negative is hunger for power. Another pitfall is an over-dependence on our minds. The area our mental power comes from is higher spiritually than the physical world, but to rise to the worlds of Spirit beyond the mental, every Soul must eventually surrender its attachment to its mind. Getting caught up in assembling "information" can keep Soul mired in the lower worlds.

Soul is a vehicle for Spirit. Soul can remain an immature, self-centered being of little or no help to Spirit in running events of even the lower worlds. Or Soul can grow into a mature spiritual being, taking its place as a spiritual helper where Spirit can best use its assistance.

Living here on Earth in the classroom of positive and negative energy is an important way for us to mature as spiritual beings.

A spiritual teacher I respect greatly has said, "The highest form of creativity is being positive." Whenever I am positive, I create an upswell of love in my heart, which uplifts everything I do. Being negative immediately begins tearing down my work, and sometimes the efforts of those around me.

I tell myself to accept the negative part of life in the physical as the teacher it is meant to be while working to be positive as often as possible.

46

PASSIONS, VIRTUES, AND NEUTRALITY

A MAP THROUGH THE MIRE

D o your passions sweep you away?

In my twenties, I thought the more passionately I lived life, the more I was alive. I ignored the wisdom of moderation and indulged whenever I could in work, art, sex, drinking, anger, laughter, and breaking the rules. Gradually my passionate outbursts became more subdued yet remained costly.

What are the passions? For me, passions are upswings in emotional intensity, which often feel productive but usually have a destructive underside.

The names of the passions vary from person to person. A spiritual teaching I feel in harmony with calls them The Five Passions of the Mind: Anger, Lust, Greed, Attachment, and Vanity—in no particular order.

Do any of these qualities play a role in your life? Do

they build or tear down your health, relationships, well-being, and personal growth?

Are you better off being a colorless person who is afraid to feel anything or a passionate person who deeply feels the world and its pain? Either extreme has its pitfalls. Is there a midpoint where we can be more in harmony with ourselves and better service to life?

I have experienced a middle path that helps me navigate my mind's passions, but it is elusive. For years I would find a good footing one morning, then by the afternoon have again swept myself away by fueling one or more passions.

For me, this middle path is neutrality. Being neutral about something does not mean I am disinterested or not involved. Being neutral means I have taken my opinion about how I think things should work and surrendered it to Spirit. This attitude helps me be at my best whenever I can.

Being neutral sounds simple to me as I describe it, yet it isn't easy to practice. Slowly, v-e-r-y slowly, I am getting better at reminding myself to be neutral in the heat of the moment. Where I put my attention is the first step. Wanting to be a particular way and then becoming this way involve different levels of self-mastery for me.

Another way to neutralize one or more passions is to develop our virtues or the side of ourselves that turns a particular negative into a positive. Again, the words I have learned to use are what works best for me. Use your descriptions of passions and virtues if they work better for you. For me, Grace is the virtue that best neutralizes Anger; Discrimination saves me from Lust; Gratitude opens my heart and frees me from Greed; Charity releases me from the heaviness of Attachment; and Humility saves me the embarrassment of Vanity.

As I write about virtues and passions, I am reminded of the preaching at my grandparent's church. Every path has truth. However, we grow stale if we think we have the whole truth while in the human state and if we fail to update what truth is for us as we gain experience.

One passion can uplift—the passion for Spirit (God by any name), no matter how you chose to express it. As with any passion, it is very easy to delude ourselves into thinking our will is more important than Spirit's.

As we neutralize our passions, we will gradually experience a state of wonder, feeling Spirit come through us in a way it has been unable to do before. Evolving into this new state of being will uplift our lives and the lives of those around us.

47

WATCH YOUR DREAMS

A WINDOW TO THE HIGHER WORLDS

In the second grade, I became determined to "wake-up" in my dreams. After several nights of going to sleep repeating to myself, "I will wake up in my dream," I did. I was at school in my normal classroom in the dream, though it looked somewhat different. I stood in front of my teacher's desk near the door. Suddenly I thrust my fist in the air and yelled, "This is a dream!"

Satisfied that I had accomplished my purpose, I abandoned any further efforts to become conscious in my dreams.

Four years later, I spent a winter wondering if I was dreaming when I was awake and if, when I was dreaming, was I truly awake. No one, including my father, had any answers to my questions, so I dropped the subject.

Today I know more about dreaming than I did then.

I have done enough work with dreams that, coupled with hearing many other people's experiences, I know some of what is possible through dreams. However, I have never committed myself to the project with the unwavering dedication that I had during the second grade.

For me today, dreams are the readiest doorway to the inner, higher worlds of Spirit. Souls live in these worlds as surely as we live here in the physical. When our physical bodies die, we, as Soul, go to one of these inner and higher worlds to review this lifetime and to then prepare for our next lifetime, wherever that may be.

Remember, I do not ask you to believe what I believe or experience just because I say it. Even if you had my identical experiences, you would probably see life at least a little differently than I do. There are as many techniques for exploring our dream worlds as there are people. Later I will share some examples.

Through our dreams, we gradually gain guidance for our daily lives. My step-by-step process includes declaring my spiritual growth to be important and then actively working at understanding my dreams. Spiritual awareness comes to each of us as we earn it and leaves us just as surely if we abuse it.

Dreams are filtered. We—our higher selves, Soul—filter the content of our dreams to avoid needless shock and upset. If you had killed and eaten numerous small children from a neighboring tribe in a past life, your higher self would undoubtedly protect you from this awareness until you were strong enough to deal with it and until the awareness could help you grow. Most of our past life activities were, thankfully, not this overt.

Dreams can provide insights into our daily situations if we learn how to interpret them. I feel most comfortable looking at the feelings and events in my dreams as having meaning unique to me. Some dream researchers feel there is a universal system of meaning in all dreams. Since dream scholars have assigned different meanings to the same "universal" symbols or events, I am skeptical. Rushing water in my dreams may not have the same meaning for me as it does for you. If dreams interest you, make a study of the field, and more importantly, your dreams.

The best way to learn about ourselves through our dreams is to keep a dream journal. We need to be dedicated. Waking up in the middle of the night to record a dream is much harder to do at 3:00 am than to plan the night before. Some people keep a small tape recorder by their bed. Other people must be careful not to disturb their spouse and slip out of bed, going to another room to make their notes. However you accomplish this feat, if you do record your dreams, review them periodically. The patterns and insights you see unfolding over time will likely amaze you.

If you have difficulty remembering your dreams, do two things. One, do not worry. Everybody goes through periods of not remembering dreams. The period may last for a few days or as long as decades. Not remembering our dreams may be caused by something simple like what we ate or needing fresh air before bed, or could result from a deeper issue, such as an unlearned inner world lesson. And, two, trying any technique you can think of or hear about. What works today may not work next week. The opposite may also be true. Retrying techniques at a later time may have positive results.

One technique that has helped me is to write this partial sentence in my dream journal before I go to sleep: "Last night I dreamed...." The next morning I begin to complete the sentence as if I had remembered a dream. If you try this, you may find a dream suddenly popping into your mind when you think you had no dreams to remember. Give this technique a month before moving on.

One December morning, I woke up with a strong memory of moving into a new apartment in my dreams. What made an impression was the unshakable feeling that this was going to happen in my physical world. The apartment was all white, large, all-new, empty, "up," and waiting for me. I lived then in a small ground-floor apartment in Waikiki. Financially, I was struggling to pay my rent. Moving seemed out of the question. I pushed the dream out of my mind, yet it lingered.

Sixteen months later, I had a similar dream. I was in no better shape financially and wondered what was going on. In six weeks, my income surged, and I moved into my new apartment within days. This apartment was on the second floor, all white, all-new, much larger than my old apartment, and had been empty since my earlier dream.

At the time of my first dream, I was pulling together a loan application for a borrower who was in foreclosure. I knew his condo had been recently renovated and that he was living with his fiancé in her home. I found a private lender who made this borrower a loan to get him out of trouble. But the borrower fell behind again on his payments. At the same time as my second dream, the borrower called the investor, without my knowing about it, and proposed that the investor buy the apartment from him to avoid another foreclosure. The investor bought the apartment, then ask me if I knew anyone who wanted to rent it.

I saw the apartment for the first time and realized it matched the one in my dreams. Even more surprising to me was suddenly being able to afford it.

This dream experience is typical for me of what I can learn in the dream state if I am willing to be open and look for guidance. Most of what I have learned from dreams has to do with my behavior and the underlying causes and effects of different situations, rather than advance warnings of changes in my outer life.

Dreams of guidance can occur when awake, too. These are called Waking Dreams. Several years ago, I let myself get very angry with a business client. I was right in my complaints, the client had not kept his word, but my anger threatened our fragile relationship. That afternoon as I got out of my car, the car door closed on me, and the edge of the glass poked me in the back. I was not injured, but it got my attention. Because I had been working on my awareness of Waking Dreams, I asked inwardly, "OK, what does this mean?" In a flash, I had an inner knowingness that the door closing on me was a reminder that my anger was "stabbing me in the back." With this new awareness, I called the client and apologized. I have remembered vividly this feeling of stabbing myself in the back since then, often reminding me to check my anger.

Here are two ways we can gain more awareness through our dreams. If you have the discipline and are so motivated, make a study of your dreams. If you are curious about how Spirit guides our everyday lives, pay attention to daily events and get in the habit of asking, "What does this mean?" when something catches your attention. You may wait a while before your first inner realization. Anything worthwhile takes practice and patience.

If you wish to know more about yourself and the worlds of Spirit, try the following technique. When you lay down at night, just before you are ready to fall asleep, ask silently to be taken to that place in the inner worlds where you have earned the right to go, where you can find the answers you need to take your next step.

Who will you ask? Any spiritual leader you feel comfortable with and trust. Start with "Spirit," if you wish. Asking for guidance is one way to avoid unnecessary problems. Many spiritual teachers no longer occupy physical bodies but are available for the asking to guide us in our learning.

Dreams and Waking Dreams are a way to know more about ourselves and our lives. More awareness does not always mean a more comfortable life, but it does give us more opportunities.

48

LOVE

IS ALL THERE IS

I ate my lunch alone, often at a health food store. Tired from too many people needing too much of me at work, I was happy for the time to myself. One day I had just sat down when a man asked if I was reading the paper on my table. I looked at him and looked at my still-folded paper lying by my tray of food. "I just bought it," I said. "I imagine I am going to read it." He apologized profusely and backed away.

What did I do? In that moment, I chose power over love. I could have used the moment to share the paper with this man. Sometimes I do share a newspaper, but usually not. In this way, I am selfish. I am not able to open easily and be loving about sharing my paper when asked. I use power to control my newspaper, so I can read exactly what I want when I want.

I can rationalize my actions. I did have a "right" to my paper, but I cannot change the reality that I chose power in that moment. I could have chosen love and still kept my paper. Later as he left, I smiled at the man, but a small place in my heart sat selfishly saying, "No, you cannot have my paper." I had filled that corner of my heart with power.

Most spiritual teachings are supposedly based on Divine Love. In subtle and not-so-subtle ways, many of these different paths attempt to control how their members think. Controlling others is using power.

The spiritual teaching I feel most at home with says we exist because of Spirit's Love for us. Spirit's Love causes Soul to exist. The teaching also emphasizes that each person's inner and outer experiences are valid for them. No written word, no spiritual leader can tell me what is truth for me. That was the principle that allowed me to get to know the teaching. Some of the path's teachings echo what I have experienced. Other parts of the teachings ring true in my heart. I have not run across any declared principles of this path that feel untrue to me, but the ones which I do not know about yet, well, I just do not know...yet.

For a long time, I have felt there is more power in Divine Love than there is in power itself. If this is so, some people will say, "Then why are there so many bad things happening in this world? Divine Love should stomp out the misuses of power." This is too simple an approach. To understand even a little of what is going on in our world, I keep in mind these principles that echo true to me:

1. We each create and recreate our worlds and experiences by the choices we make now and have made in our past,
2. We are here to mature spiritually,
3. Our physical bodies are temporary,
4. Our true self, Soul, is a naturally happy being who never dies and cannot be harmed,
5. Pain is caused primarily by our resistance to hurts which will leave us if we do not hold onto them,
6. We grow through experience--all kinds of experience, and,
7. There are as many paths home to God as there are people.

The tricky part of dealing with power comes when I —or any of us—try to direct it. The power of Divine Love is the trickiest. We cannot direct any power. We can only fool ourselves. What we do may not come back to us for a number of lifetimes, but it is coming back. The miseries in our lives today come from past attempts to direct power. Some of us, like me, learn slowly.

When I have tried to redirect a strong flow of love coming through me for my purposes, invariably, I get burned. This folly of mine feels like trying to shake hands with a laser.

If we exist because of Spirit's Love for us, then Love must be all there is. A more practical approach for me in this world is that Love is all there is...that counts.

Years ago, I sat in an attorney's office, discussing his need to refinance a condo he owned. I listened as he described his problematic history with this apartment. He had purchased the property to help a friend who could not close her escrow. The friend had walked out on the deal, leaving him with an apartment he never wanted. His current tenant was not fulfilling either of his promises to renovate the place or pay partial rent, adding cash flow and repair problems to the attorney's list of woes.

All through the attorney's monologue about how B-A-D the situation was surrounding the apartment, I kept seeing how he was looking at the experience only through his mind and wallet. He apparently had not opened his heart to let Spirit have a chance to go to work. This was my inner awareness. I did not know if it accurately described the whole picture, and I did not sit in judgment of this man. When he finished, he said for the fifth time, "I just do not know what to do with this apartment. Everything I try turns bad."

A voice inside of me cried out, "Give this situation some love. Just stand back and open your heart. Keep a rein on your mind and your checkbook while you allow love to dissolve the knots of conflict."

Feeling full of awareness and love, I said to the attorney, "Have you tried just...loving the apartment?" The good rapport we had built up over the past thirty minutes shuddered. He looked at me, his mouth half-open for what felt like a long time. I knew I had blown the interview. He snorted and mumbled and said something not quite intelligible. My smile faded.

Perhaps there was good that happened that day. I did not accomplish my goal of completing his loan application. The attorney did not appear to have understood my point about love. We parted ten minutes later with him muttering that he would call me when he had his financials together. He never finished nor canceled the loan application I had taken, and I did not hear from him again.

So what did I learn that day? Being foolish was not new for me, but I still remember the look on the attorney's face and have used that experience to wait a little longer before introducing new elements to business transactions.

I felt I had offered a gift to the attorney, and he was not ready for it. If I was deluding myself, it would not be the first time. I would have liked to have his business, would have liked to have seen him a happier man, but survived without either. I took a risk. Once away from his office, I grinned at my craziness.

If I had taken the risk to rise above my little stresses in the restaurant, I could have been gracious to the man who wanted my paper and therefore been a little happier with myself. I would have let more love shine through me.

The more love we let shine through ourselves, the more love we have to share and experience.

49

SPIRITUAL EXERCISE

SING HU

Many spiritual teachings talk about the Light. Some paths speak of the Sound. A few teachings work with both the Light and Sound as the way Spirit manifests itself in the lower worlds, including the physical world.

The light and sound in our everyday world are reflections of this inner Light and Sound. Ever catch a flash of light—perhaps a twinkle of blue—out of the corner of your eye? Have you had a ringing in your ears or heard birds, bees, rushing wind, or other sounds of nature when no one else did? If so, you might have been experiencing a psychotic episode or suffering from tinnitus, but the chances are good you were hearing the inner Sound of Spirit.

If you sit quietly by yourself with your eyes closed and look gently into the area a little above your eyebrows between your eyes, you will be gazing into what is called by many the Third Eye. This area is where our spiritual vision can open to the inner worlds. What people experience when looking into the Third Eye varies dramatically. Some people have little, if any, awareness except looking into the back of their eyelids. Other people see colors swirl, images form, and sometimes whole worlds unfold before them. Still other people have experiences with Spiritual Guides who can exist in the physical world and the inner worlds at the same time or chose to no longer occupy a physical body.

Whatever your experience, it will probably not be as clear as I have just described. With people so used to watching movies and television, giving validity to more subtle experiences are difficult. When I sit quietly and focus on my Third Eye, my inner experiences are not like watching television. Most people do not have technicolor inner experiences, but some do. We each vary in how we are best able to perceive Spirit. I am better at recognizing the hand of Spirit in everyday activities than having Hollywood extravaganzas on the inner.

Many different sounds can be chanted, sung softly, or sung loudly. Although appearing to be just sound made by our vocal cords and mouths, different sounds have different effects on us and our world around us.

Imagine yourself sitting quietly in a sunny room on a spring morning, playing with a kitten, while you listen to a soft wind blowing in the window and birds singing outside. Into the scene, imagine a dozen men with jackhammers ripping up the sidewalk outside your window. Sound can have a noticeable effect on our lives. The sound of some people's voices is more harmonious to us than other people's voices. Why? Sound, and which sounds we are in harmony with, resonate throughout our lives. In just this way, the sounds we sing or listen to can gradually change our consciousness.

The sound I like to sing is HU. I have learned that HU is a very old name for Spirit. Reportedly the sound of HU (pronounced like the man's name, Hugh) is of a very high spiritual nature and can uplift anyone singing it. My experience of singing HU has been more than was reported.

To sing HU, I take ten to twenty minutes each day, often at the same time of day, sit quietly and comfortably in a room where I will not be disturbed, close my eyes, breathe a few times deeply, then on my outward breath sing softly, "HHHHUUUUU." Over and over again, I sing, "HHHHUUUUU." Usually, my voice softens until I am no longer singing, but I hear the HU in my inner hearing. Sometimes I fade out of a soft HU with my physical voice and into a loud roaring HU on the inner, as if I have stepped into a waterfall of sound.

Singing HU washes away my negative feelings. Singing HU helps gently raise my outlook to a higher spiritual viewpoint. Singing HU helps open my heart, allowing the Love of Spirit to flow through more freely. Singing HU helps open my spiritual vision, sometimes leading to an inner experience with the Light and

Sound and occasionally with one of the Spiritual Guides I work with best.

My mind sometimes chatters when I sit down to sing HU, and that is fine. Let your mind wander where it wishes. After a while, you will learn to guide your mind away from chatter to calmness or a contemplation topic. Sometimes I am able to step around my mind's chatter as I would step around children playing on the beach.

After singing HU for a few minutes, when the HU falls quiet, I sometimes gently focus on a subject or question or spiritual teaching and quietly contemplate. I let whatever I have focused on roll gently through my mind. This is not a time to be controlling anything. Contemplation opens us to our inner wisdom. Spiritualizing our contemplations by singing HU opens us more profoundly and in a more balanced way to the Love of Spirit.

During a contemplation, in the dream state, or in everyday life, if you find yourself frightened or upset, sing HU out loud or silently and ask Spirit for help. The help you receive may or may not be what you want, but if you keep your mind and heart open, you may be amazed at what happens.

Sound and Light and singing HU are nondenominational. People practicing many different `teachings use HU to uplift themselves spiritually. When you feel lost or are not sure which way to turn, think of the Sound as your homing signal, which will lead you out of the dark forest to the warmth of your home. The Light will help illuminate each step you take so you can avoid unnecessary troubles on your way home.

Even when we do not feel lost and unsure, singing HU can clarify our next step.

50

HOW TO HEAL A RELATIONSHIP

A SPIRITUAL EXERCISE THAT WORKS

My wife and I met in very tangled circumstances. Sweetie—as I now call her —answered my singles ad, but for her sister, who was visiting the islands. We had an hour-long conversation in which I learned she was in an unhappy relationship and that I liked her a lot. I had been down the confusing road of being in a relationship with someone already in a relationship. I was not looking for a repeat of the pain or karmic complications.

One evening the three of us met for dinner at a local Thai restaurant. I sat across from them. Communication was interesting. They are from a different culture than mine and are not native speakers of English. Sweetie taught English in her home country, but her sister's English was very limited. Sweetie served as the translator for her sister at dinner, so I had to look at both of them a lot. I worked hard to divide eye contact and conversation equally between these two lovely women, but my heart was focused on the woman I would marry 17 months later.

Marriage was not in my plans then. Getting involved with someone already involved was even less inviting. But Sweetie was so wonderfully inviting. She was not trying to invite me into her life. She was just being herself. I could have looked into her eyes forever.

The evening ended awkwardly, however. We were asked to leave the restaurant after ordering only pupus (appetizers) and sitting talking intensely for three hours. I forgot about ordering main dishes, and the restaurant was packed.

We found ourselves on the sidewalk talking and laughing. I was feeling a little strained. Later I found out they thought I was strange for not ordering more food and wondered if I was tight with money.

I went home, stirred up, confused, and wanting to put the evening behind me. I knew there was no attraction between her sister and me. And I knew I did not want to get involved with Sweetie because of her situation.

But I did want to get involved with Sweetie.

I called her a few days later but missed her. She called back later, but I was busy. Finally, after a week went by, we talked, and I asked her if I could have lunch with her alone to talk about her sister. She agreed.

The next week, on a Thursday, we met for lunch. I told her that I was not attracted to her sister, and I was sorry about that. I also offered to be her friend. These words did not come tumbling out. I struggled for half the lunch to explain. Sweetie was very graceful...and oh so charming to me.

I learned her significant other would not help her buy a car. She had the money and disliked driving his SUV into town from the north shore for work every day.

After lunch, we went car shopping in the rain. A few days later, we looked at car lots again.

Over the next few weeks, we saw each other several times, and a closeness began to build. Sweetie's sister and mother lived in town because her partner was not kind to them. Sweetie often stayed overnight with her mom and sister. One night she stayed with me.

We then began a two-month dance about whether she was going to leave her partner. Their fighting had increased and her happiness at her home was dissolving. She had entanglements with him, though, which were not easily cast off.

I began going through my personal hell. Wanting her, needing her, I still knew that loving meant giving freedom. My spiritual goals and my emotional neediness clashed horribly. I was doing it again—in a relationship with someone already in a relationship. Damn!

We roller-coastered through the next few weeks. One evening just before we were leaving my apartment, Sweetie told me she thought she should stay with her partner for a while longer for reasons which had nothing to do with her heart. I was crushed. As we drove in her car to her mother's small home, I just could not stand the pain. I pulled over and stopped the car. "I just can't take this anymore," I cried. I got out of the car, left the motor running, and took off walking back to my place.

I was blind with pain and rage. The rage primarily came because I could not stay with my pain. I was upset that Sweetie was going to stay with her partner. I did not see the balancing energy of her doing what she felt was best for herself.

As I walked home and cooled down a little, I wondered if Sweetie would come looking for me. Boy, was I wrong. Later that evening, when I called her to apologize, she would not even speak to me. She also would not talk to me the next day when she was at work. After her workday was over, I showed up at her mom's apartment with a double bouquet of roses. I felt very relieved to see her car in the drive.

The roses at least got me in the door. I apologized with every ounce of my heart. I felt horrible. I had abandoned her. I had left her sitting in her car on the side of the road. She had been pissed. She thought I was nuts for just taking off walking. She had gone home later that evening and had a huge fight with her partner. She had told him about me. She had told him what she then told me: she was leaving us both.

My world ended with her words. My heart filled with nothingness. I looked into her eyes and saw her hurt and a steely determination to stop being with anyone who caused her grief.

I left crushed—my own doing. I drove home slowly. I sat at the desk, which served as my dining table for a long time. The phone was silent, of course. Sweetie would not be calling me.

Then I called Arlean. She was a dear friend with a lot of spiritual wisdom. She knew about Sweetie but had not met her. Arlean and I talked for a while. She asked me a lot of questions about how I felt about Sweetie and the details of her situation. She then told me about a spiritual exercise she uses when she has a problem with someone near her. She talked about the troubles she had had with her daughter when she was growing up. Arlean offered me the following technique:

"Sit quietly when you are alone and gently put your focus on the person you are having a problem with. Then say the person's name out loud and follow with: 'The God in me loves the God in you.' Do not say this to the person or try to influence them. This is a neutral statement that will help raise your energy to a higher level and will also help the other person because you are removing some of your inner tangles from their lives—at least for the time being. You can also say this silently to yourself. Whether out loud or silently, repeat it for as long as you wish."

I thanked Arlean, and we hung up. I wondered about what she had said, but not for too long. Sitting in my chair in the middle of my apartment, I began saying softly, "Sweetie, the God in me loves the God in you." I repeated it softly and loudly for a long time. I slipped into singing HU, then into quiet contemplation.

I awoke the next morning in bed without my contacts in my eyes. I had no memory of going to bed or taking out my contacts. I called Sweetie at work. She had taken the day off. I called her cell phone. She answered. I asked her if I could come to see her. She said yes. Her tone of voice was neutral. My heart wanted to soar, but I held it in check.

I drove to her Mom's home and knocked on the door. Sweetie answered. I took her hands in mine, still standing in the doorway. I told her how so very, very sorry I was to have been so stupid and that I would never leave her again unless she wanted me to do so.

Sweetie looked at me, into my eyes, for what felt like a long time, then smiled warmly and said, "Why don't you come in."

You can guess what a happy camper I was!

Have Sweetie and I had some problems since then? Sure. But not too many. In the next two years, I learned first-hand the guiding principles of our marriage: harmony is more important than being right, and love means giving freedom.

I also treasure the gift Arlean gave me. If you find yourself wishing to heal a relationship you have, then I whole-heartedly suggest you say to yourself, as often as you wish, the person's name followed with "The God in me loves the God in you."

51

COXSACKIE B4

I WAS NOT CRAZY!

I n my twenties, I fed my passions, as mentioned earlier. I spent my thirties recovering my health from my twenties lifestyle. When my forties began, I had moved to Honolulu and was feeling better, though my healing was not complete.

What was going on? How to fix myself? I chased these two quests for decades. No western doctor could find anything wrong with me in my blood work or after test upon test.

I tried many alternative approaches. At first, I tried everything I could at once, then saw that I was repeating my pattern of going to extremes. I looked back on a 30 day fast in San Francisco that had left me with dangerously low electrolyte levels as a warning sign to seek the middle path. Even though I had regained a significant amount of my health—and had avoided killing myself by depleting my potassium only to the near fatal range—I saw that I needed to take my healing step by step. I also looked inward and focused on developing my inner dialogue for guidance.

In Honolulu, I have gone through two of my behavior cycles with resulting lows. Thankfully as my awareness has opened, I have acquired some common sense and did not plunge as low as earlier in my life.

Years and steps later, a mortgage client suggested I see Dr. O. We had gotten to know each other well enough she knew about my continuing physical challenges. I thanked her and sat with the referral for two days, then called Dr. O's office to make an appointment. My client friend had been very detailed about how much Dr. O had helped her and other people she knew.

I learned that Doc, as I call him, has a unique method of diagnosing and treating. He also is an open-hearted and delightful man, traits that enhance every visit to see him.

Doc's method analyzes 22 areas of the body for imbalances. He then tests to find which combination of supplements and remedies will balance any given area. He found I had plenty to work on.

His principal finding was that I had a virus named Coxsackie B4 buried in 7 of my body's 22 areas. Hopeful, I began his 10-week course of treatment. Almost three months later, just after week 10's treatment, I felt my always-present flu-like symptoms leave my body. I rejoiced! Soon though, I realized the physical stresses left by years of this virus had created other imbalances. More to work on.

I learned that Coxsackie B4 had been identified in the 1960s in a small town in eastern New York on the Hudson River named Coxsackie, New York. I had my first weird flu in January 1980 after running around northern Indiana for the holidays. This flu cycled through me literally 100s of times over the next thirty five years. I had proved to be an excellent host with my balls-to-the-wall lifestyle. A "pesky virus" most people could shake in a couple of weeks, the Coxsackie strain is not detectable or treatable with western medicine.

I was not crazy after all. There had been something physically wrong with me all this time…and it had a name! After chasing my tail for so many years, I was relieved.

With Dr. O's treatment, I am living Coxsackie B4 free, though still dealing with the impact on my body of having this virus flare-up so many times.

From my journey through San Francisco's mental health system, I experienced how uplifting the years of professional help turned out to be. My life has improved greatly by working on—and sometimes through—my emotional issues, and I am grateful for it.

Had I been diagnosed with Coxsackie B4 in the early 1980s and successfully treated for it before my emotional work, I might still be running amok.

52

EVERYTHING HAS VALUE

SOME PATHS ARE SHORTER

I have shared some of my experiences and beliefs with you, given you too many opinions I imagine, and suggested ways to uplift your life. Hopefully, I have posed some thought-provoking questions, perhaps helped you find ways to open your heart, and maybe simulated you to push the envelope of your spiritual awareness.

Whatever you have experienced from reading these pages, I hope you will keep what works for you and forget the rest. This is how we learn. Some of us move through life in this way more easily than others.

I tend to either immediately reject what I hear, read, and see—or take it all in too deeply and then have a hard time letting go of what does not work for me. I get my waste products and my nutrients all mixed up. Having learned this part of myself, I now weave more easily through the world's outer stimulations. The chatter of my attachments, though, can still get in the way of learning from the inner worlds.

I hope you have an easier time with your growing than I sometimes do with mine.

Experience is our teacher. Learning to rise above the pleasure and pain of a situation and seeing that our experiences, no matter how they feel, are teaching us freedom is a great step. If we attach ourselves to pleasure or avoid pain, we trap ourselves. Enjoy your pleasure, be smart enough to limit your pain, and learn to welcome what comes your way with the graceful awareness that you have created it for your spiritual growth. The better you master this principle, the lighter and higher your steps will become.

Some paths are longer; some paths are more direct in our journey home to God. Everyday choices are our keys to uplifting our lives.

May The Blessings Be!

About the Author

BC embraces life's adventures by focusing more on what he is doing than what he has. Relying on spiritual awareness, often called intuition, helps him to see the hidden lessons behind everyday encounters. Learning (still!) that ignoring this inner guidance often makes the road rougher to travel, he accepts opportunities to unfold however they come.

When asked about his writing, he explains, *"Forty years ago, I found I had little to write about. Ten years later, I began to develop my writer's voice."* Today BC lives in Honolulu with his lovely wife Sweetie, delving into his personal experiences and imagination through his writing.

www.bccowling.com

www.ingramcontent.com/pod-product-compliance
Lightning Source LLC
Chambersburg PA
CBHW031545040426
42452CB00006B/192